The Little Book of New Mum Feelings

Praise for *The Little Book of Calm for New Mums*

'A beautiful and informative companion of a book that'll help keep you grounded and present in the moments that often feel overwhelming. I found myself noting uplifting quotes I know will come in useful as mantras when needed. Anna has always been, and continues to be, a woman I take so much wisdom from. Her compassion and guidance for a mother's mental health are invaluable'

Giovanna Fletcher

'This lovely book offers little gems of support, helping us to be in the moment and reminding us to direct some of our maternal love to ourselves. Anna Mathur's empathy and wise insight make this an essential read for new mums'

Fearne Cotton

'Like having a reassuring chat with a wise friend, Anna's kind and grounding words provide the perfect companion for new mums making sense of their vast – and at times, conflicting! – feelings'

Sarah Turner, aka the Unmumsy Mum

'A tender, real and uplifting book. The voice of comfort and reassurance, Anna skilfully mothers the mother – not advice and parenting hacks, but the healing words every mother needs to hear. So many actionable gems giving access to peace in the moment, no matter how tough it gets; healing permission to feel the full gamut of emotion; and, most importantly, the healthy strategies to deal with it. Page by page, Anna unlocks our capacity for self-compassion. In reading this book I feel heard and understood. This is a shared journey, and I don't feel alone any more. Mum-guilt slides from my shoulders'

Suzy Reading, chartered psychologist and bestselling author of *The Self-Care Revolution*

'Anna's *Little Book of Calm for New Mums* feels like such a reassuring and necessary companion for motherhood. Broken down into the feelings and emotions that are sometimes hard to decipher when we're in the throes of parenting, Anna has such a wonderful way of bringing comfort, clarity and insight to many of the overwhelming challenges new mums can find themselves up against. The book is accessible and written with the wisdom of an expert but the love and compassion of a friend, and I think that's what makes it such a valuable resource on the rollercoaster of motherhood'

Hollie de Cruz, bestselling author of *Your Baby, Your Birth* and *Motherhood Your Way*

'This book is going to be a lifeline for new mums. Anna has an incredible gift of offering not only her professional expertise, but also love, perspective and compassion – often in just one sentence. A much-needed gift to the world'

Zoe Blaskey, founder of Motherkind

'Such a brilliant idea for a book. Anna's punchy chapters are like bite-sized pep talks which make it incredibly accessible and unbelievably comforting for overwhelmed new mums. Like getting the most brilliant advice from your wisest and warmest friend. I wish I'd had this book when I had newborn'

Ellie-Jane Taylor, actor, comedian, TV presenter and author of *My Child and Other Mistakes*

'Anna's a consistent source of relatable, practical and reassuring advice when it comes to navigating the mental health challenges of motherhood. Packed with soothing words to validate the messy emotions that come with being a mum, along with useful quick tips to help bring calm to the chaos, this book is a gem of support. A must-have for every bookshelf and baby-changing bag!'

Molly Forbes, TV presenter and author of *Body Happy Kids*

'A comforting and reassuring book to help you navigate those tricky early years'

Helen Thorn, one half of the Scummy Mummies

The Little Book of New Mum Feelings

An A–Z of Warm Words
for Every Motherhood
Emotion

Anna Mathur

PENGUIN LIFE

UK | USA | Canada | Ireland | Australia
India | New Zealand | South Africa

Penguin Life is part of the Penguin Random House group of companies
whose addresses can be found at global.penguinrandomhouse.com.

First published as *The Little Book of Calm for New Mums* 2022
Published as *The Little Book of New Mum Feelings* 2023
001

Set in 12/18pt TT Commons Classic Book
Typeset by Jouve (UK), Milton Keynes
Printed and bound in Great Britain by Clays Ltd, Elcograf S.p.A.

The authorized representative in the EEA is Penguin Random House
Ireland, Morrison Chambers, 32 Nassau Street, Dublin D02 YH68

A CIP catalogue record for this book is available from the British Library

ISBN: 978-0-241-67014-9

www.greenpenguin.co.uk

About Anna

I'm a psychotherapist, a bestselling author and a mum of two boys and a girl, living in Surrey. I am passionate about taking therapy out of the therapy room. I love sharing my personal and professional experience to support fellow mums through motherhood.

Over the years, I have realized just how much we judge and criticize ourselves for feeling anything other than 'happy and grateful'. Sure, babies bring us much gratitude and joy but also a boatload of other feelings too.

It can often feel like a vulnerable thing to do, to start honest conversations about the highs and lows, the mundane and the challenges along the way in early motherhood. Judgement, shame and guilt are hurdles preventing us from connecting authentically with others. My hope is that, as you read these pages, you'll feel heard, understood and increasingly confident in both facing and sharing the feelings of motherhood. For your feelings are no reflection on the love you have for your baby, and the sooner we find compassion and understanding for ourselves, the more confidence we will find in seeking it from, and offering it to, others.

So, wave goodbye to destructive self-judgement, and say hello to life-affirming self-compassion.

How to Use This Book

If I were to sit with you on your sofa, make you a cup of tea and support you through the feelings that come with being a new mum, these would be the things I'd say.

Whether you need some quick grounding or compassion, or you want to untangle a feeling, flick to a page for a moment of support and calm.

You'll find a quick takeaway mantra should you be tight on time, which you can repeat for some comfort in the moment.

You'll also find an action tip and then I'll suggest three other topics you can flick to, should you want to explore things more deeply.

Contents

Angry   1
Anxious   6
Baby Blues   14
Bad Day   20
Bored   24
Comparing Myself   29
Crying Baby   36
Depressed   44
Don't Feel Good Enough   51
Envious   56
Exhausted   61
Feel Like a Burden   72
Grateful   79
Grieving   84
Guilty   92
Hormonal   98
Information Overload   104
Insomnia   110
Intrusive Thoughts   118
Irritable   124
Judged   129
Lonely   134
Loud Inner Critic   144

Missing My Old Life   149
Need Space   156
Overwhelmed   161
Panicking   168
Procrastinating   173
Resentful   180
Routine Anxiety   186
Self-care   192
Sensitive to Noise   198
Social Anxiety   203
Social Media Overload   211
Suicidal   217
Tearful   224
Touched Out   228
Traumatized   233
Unsolicited Advice   240
Unwell   248
Who Am I?   253
Winging It!   260

Final Note from Anna   269
Helpful Contacts   271
Acknowledgements   285

angry

angry

Anger and rage point to unexpressed, unvalidated emotion, and repeatedly unmet needs

Sometimes I feel like the inside of my core holds some red-hot lava. It can lie dormant, or it can be bubbling away, coming out in spurts of irritation at something that wouldn't normally bother me that much. Perhaps a badly timed doorbell, a message requiring something of me in a moment I'm busy,

1

something dropped or scraped. Or the lava can erupt, flooding out in a physical and emotional way that makes me want to throw or break something, run away or scream. I've roared like a lioness in my kitchen when I've hit breaking point after a day of tantrums and screaming.

Anger is a very active emotion, and an outburst can lead to feelings of shame and guilt. So, what do you do with anger and rage when you're a mum? It's an emotion so many of us, including myself, feel an increase of in motherhood!

Here are my three approaches to when you feel the rage:

1 Compassion

Always start with compassion. You are not a bad person. I repeat, you are not a bad person for feeling a normal, human emotion. A taboo one perhaps (I'm trying to change that), but a normal one. There will be a reason you feel this way. You don't need to shame and criticize yourself; you need gentleness and comfort.

Anger and rage are often pointers to unexpressed, unvalidated emotion, and repeatedly unmet needs. You have a baby and it's likely that in loving them, as you do so well, you've forgotten to care for yourself too. In meeting their needs, you've overlooked yours; in responding to their feelings, you've nudged yours aside. This isn't about 'fault' or doing it wrong, it's just a common narrative we so often live to – that to love is to overlook ourselves.

2 Talk it out

If you feel hurt by a situation or a person, and are holding those feelings down, you deserve

to verbalize them and have them heard.
Resentment and hurt can fuel this simmering
feeling of anger and rage, especially when
you feel something unjust has happened to
you. Even if that person isn't open to
conversation, or the circumstance can't be
changed, thrashing those feelings out with
someone who is kind and supportive adds
validation to your experience and can help
you feel heard and justified.

3 Identify your feelings and needs

Much of the anger and rage I experience is
down to the fact that I've not met my own
needs for a while or have repeatedly
swallowed down my feelings so that I can
stay calm in challenging moments. I know
you likely have a need for space, rest and
quiet, which are hard to come by as a new
mum and tend to require some support from

others to enable you to get them. But if you overlook needs and feelings, they don't just disappear (as convenient as that would be) – they build.

∾ **TIP:** ∾

Find small ways to disperse feelings by verbalizing them, naming them, talking them through. And find small ways to meet and acknowledge your needs so that the pressure cooker doesn't pop.

∾

See also:
Hormonal
Irritable
Resentful

anxious

Anxiety distorts the statistics

Sometimes it doesn't take much to spark an anxiety tornado in my mind. I could be lying in bed or standing in the kitchen when a twinge in my chest, a news article or a fever take my thoughts from calm to chaos in a split second.

Suddenly, my mind rushes ahead into a future that has not and may never happen. The possibilities play out in cinematic, high-definition Technicolor in my head. My shoulders tense, my pulse rate climbs and my heart gets dragged along for the ride as it feels waves of loss and fear.

Anxiety, in and of itself, is an incredible process designed purely to save our lives. It makes us hyperalert and fills us with adrenaline so that we can fight or flee. However, the challenge comes when this life-saving alarm system is triggered not by a life-threatening risk but by our thoughts. While our mind is able to rationalize what is and what isn't truly happening, our body responds regardless.

Most of our anxieties are fear-based, and when we're tired and going through times of change and uncertainty, it's harder to coach ourselves and rationalize those thoughts. Plus you add a baby into the mix, and the concerns and worries about what could go wrong can feel endless! The stakes seem higher when love is on the line. This is why new mums may feel more anxious than perhaps they used to.

The good thing is, there is so much hope. And there are ways to slow the whirlwind of thoughts. Here are some of my favourites:

- Imagine the anxious part of you as your scared inner child, and try to reassure and comfort her.
- Remind yourself that someone else's story doesn't dictate your outcome. This one is handy for those times you hear something that has happened to someone else and, before you know it, you have put yourself in their shoes and are feeling the weight of fear and heartbreak.

- Know that anxiety distorts statistics. That twinge is most likely caused by a muscle cramp, even though you feel as if it's most certainly something more sinister.
- Ground yourself in the present when your mind is rushing ahead into the uncertainty of the future. Feel the ground under your feet, notice what is around you, the noises, sights, smells, tastes and textures. Name them to bring your awareness back from the future unknowns to the certainty of the present moment.
- Adopt a calming mantra such as 'I will cross that bridge *if* I get to it'. This one can act as a reminder that the majority of the things we fear never happen. It's also an invitation to reflect on the fact that we've crossed many challenging 'bridges' in our lives thus far.

- Try a breathing exercise that helps you. There are many to experiment with but a simple starter is to breathe in deeply to the count of four, and exhale steadily to a longer count of five or six. It signals to your body that you're safe and helps switch off the fight-or-flight response.

Finally, I want to say that feeling anxious in motherhood is so common. You're not failing, you're feeling. We are wired to protect ourselves and our babies from harm, and there are ways to calm our minds and bodies so that anxious thoughts don't run quite as wild, quite as often. Anxiety is common, but it doesn't need to be your normal.

It can be challenging to reassure yourself that 'the worst probably won't happen' after you've been through a traumatic time when the worst *did* happen. Please seek support if you feel your anxiety is overwhelming and hard to control. There is so much hope that you can regain control and headspace in time, and you deserve that.

········· **TIP:** ·········

Practise using these tools when you don't need them (as you fall asleep is a brilliant time), so that when you feel the anxiety whirlwind picking up, the techniques are familiar and easier to grab.

·········

See also:
Intrusive Thoughts
Panicking
Traumatized

Imagine the **anxious** part of you as

reassure and comfort her.

your scared inner
child,
and try to

baby

Life has just changed
immeasurably. That
is both wonderful and
overwhelmingly intense!

blues

Everyone talks about baby blues, but what exactly are they? Perhaps you've flicked to this page because you're feeling tearful and low and wondering whether it's normal. But where is the bar of normal?

Let me tell you this. There is such an expectation and assumption that once your baby is safely in your arms, you should feel wonderful, elated, utterly in love. And sure, maybe those feelings are there in abundance, or maybe they're a bit softened by sleep deprivation and the huge hormonal changes that come in the post-partum period. Maybe those lovely feelings are intermingled with 'Goodness me, what has happened to my life/my body/my identity/my relationship/my friendships?' So much changes when you have a baby, and the last thing you need is the additional pressure to feel constantly happy, both for yourself and around others.

What are baby blues?

- Experiencing low mood and mild depression shortly after having your baby
- Feeling emotional, tearful for no apparent reason, anxious, restless and irritable
- Often triggered by low energy levels and sudden shifts in hormones

I know it's not nice to feel like this, but please be gentle on yourself. Unlike the social media posts on display and the front-of-house scenes you may glimpse of other people's lives, it is utterly normal to feel a whole herd of feelings at this time. Your life has just changed immeasurably. That is both wonderful and overwhelmingly intense! Ride those waves, cry those tears, seek those hugs and cups of tea, and cuss the power of the hormones in hasty text messages to friends. How your hormones (and the comfort of your body) are making you feel is no reflection on how grateful you are to have your baby here safely.

Now, what if the fleeting baby blues turn to gloomy grey clouds that linger? I often get asked when a mum should go and seek support and my answer is always, 'If you're even asking that question, seek support because you're deserving of it.' Speak with a friend, your partner, your GP, your midwife or health visitor. Regardless of how many boxes you tick on a diagnostic list, if you're not feeling okay, please have those conversations. I've signposted some places to seek help in the Helpful Contacts section at the end of the book.

Typical symptoms of postnatal depression are:

- Difficulty bonding
- Feelings of hopelessness and not being able to cope
- Anxiety, lack of enjoyment, panic attacks, crying
- Insomnia, loss of appetite, inability to concentrate

Speaking as a mum who has had postnatal depression, I can tell you that while I thought I could keep calm and carry on, it got me nowhere but deeper into my own darkness and feelings of failure. The light came when I began to speak about it, when I reached out to those who could support, hear and help me. In time, the light flooded back into my life, and I know that, with the right support, it is possible for you too. You are not made to do this alone. Finding it hard isn't failure, it's a human response to your circumstances. We all have different histories, resources and situations, so try not to compare yours with someone else's, as their journey is not a statement of how good a mum you are.

TIP:

Keep a simple, bullet-point journal of your feelings over the space of a few weeks, so that you can keep an eye on their rhythms and fluctuations. Use your 'okay days' as a reference point and if you don't feel yourself for more than two weeks, please seek support.

See also:
Bad Day
Depressed
Hormonal

bad day

A bad moment doesn't have to mean a bad day

Eugh, I know that feeling when everything seems to be going wrong, and each thing just drags your energy levels down along with the corners of your smile.

I remember a grey day pushing the buggy down the road after a rough night. I'd forgotten the changing bag, locked myself out of the house and then got drenched by a torrent of rainwater flung over me from the wheel of a passing lorry. My internal voice had 'What a bad day' repeating on a loop.

And then I remembered how we have a choice whether to carry that attitude through the rest of the day or not. Sure, sometimes it's harder to shift gear when you're running on no sleep and things aren't going your way, but what might you do today that turns it around a little bit?

Here are some simple but powerful things that help me:

- **Gratitude** List 5–10 things that you're grateful for.
- **Download** Scribble out your feelings of frustration on a piece of paper or rant to a friend on the phone, and then imagine

walking away from that black, tangled ball of irritation.

- **Laugh and sing** Watch something that makes you laugh, tickle your baby until you are both smiling, or put your favourite song on and let your body go from stiff to moving with the beat as your endorphins rise.

- **Find a mantra to empower you** 'A bad moment doesn't have to mean a bad day' is one of mine.

- **Connect with someone** Reach out and talk to a friend who lifts your spirit.

- **Get outside** Take a breather by going for a walk around the block. Rarely do I return from a walk feeling the same as when I left.

⌁ **TIP:** ⌁

Form a small list of things that help you reframe your bad days so that you can use it as a reminder when things feel grey.

———

See also:
Angry
Baby Blues
Depressed

bored

**Gratitude brings
balance to boredom**

The Groundhog Day-ness of new motherhood
can feel so relentless at times. I have felt so
guilty for finding the mundanity of the baby
stage so . . . boring. I'd ask myself, 'But you
wanted this, why aren't you enjoying it enough?'

The thing is, telling yourself to enjoy something
that doesn't always feel that enjoyable is a way

of invalidating a valid feeling. Perhaps it feels mundane not because you don't appreciate being a mum, but because, very simply, it *is* mundane. It is relentless, it *is* boring sometimes! Try not to shame or criticize yourself for having what is a human response to the monotonous parts of motherhood.

Of course, there are the things that we cannot control, like the constant stream of washing that overflows from the washing basket the moment I've emptied it, or the fact my toddler wants to read the same story every single evening and will not be lured by any other book regardless of how many lift-up flaps it boasts or animal-noise buttons there are to press.

So, while there are things we cannot remove from the daily routine, instead let's focus for a moment on what we can do. Here are some things that help break my boredom:

- **Meeting up with other mothers** Chaos in company can shift the dynamic of your day. Doing 'the same old things' but together can add some difference while also building relationships.
- **Changing the environment** Move from the table to the picnic blanket, or camp out at a friend or family member's house for the day to get a change of scenery. Also, the different sights and smells provide different sensory interest for your baby.
- **Making time to do your 'thing'** What do you enjoy doing? What is your stress-relieving 'flow' activity of choice, or the thing that makes you smile or laugh? How can you inject some more of that into your day even if it's just in a small way?

- **Flirting with flexibility** I don't know about you, but I often feel trapped in routine, forgetting that it's okay to mix it up a bit. I tend to find myself saying 'no' to things that disrupt our fixed rhythm without taking a moment to question whether it might actually be . . . fun! Next time an opportunity arises, consider what it might be like to embrace it. What it disrupts in terms of routine, it may make up for in terms of enjoyment and breaking the boredom.

- **Talking about it** I find chatting about the boredom and finding common ground with others an important reminder that I am not alone, and that having those feelings is not something to feel ashamed of.

- **Adopting an attitude of gratitude** Finding the privilege, the beauty or the humour in the mundane certainly helps lift my mood and reminds me of the bigger picture. When I find myself focusing purely on the boredom, gratitude brings a little balance, reminding me that it sure can be boring, but it's good too.

⌒ **TIP:** ⌒

Plan at least one thing into your day that is different. Mix it up a bit, whether it's a change of scenery, company or a mix-up of your routine.

⌒

See also:
Grateful
Missing My Old Life
Procrastinating

comparing

**Comparison overlooks
the wonderful complexity
of humanness**

myself

What aspect of yourself are you comparing at the moment? Is it a decision you've made, or a way you like to do things? What are you looking for when you compare yourself with someone else? Are you hungering for confirmation that you're doing it right, or that you're good enough? Perhaps you're seeking to feel good and affirmed by what you find.

The thing is, whether the outcome of your comparison leaves you feeling better or worse, it always overlooks the true rich and wonderful complexity of your own humanness (and that of other people too). You can never be reduced down to a mere ruler against which other things and people are measured. You are so much more than what others see, as are they.

So often, comparison isn't even a fair game. It's like comparing a sheep to a pigeon and berating it for not being able to fly. We all have different backgrounds, experiences, support, resources and stories. But, most importantly, we all have a very different behind-the-scenes reality to the snapshot we often see of each other's lives.

Here are some things that might help:

- Become aware of the moments you use comparison to make statements about who you are. You might feel 'she is a more patient mother than me, therefore *I am not good enough*' or 'she is doing it like that, therefore *I must be doing it wrong*'. These statements are incredibly powerful and often resonate deeply because we tend to compare our perceived weaknesses with others' strengths.

- Remember that everything has a cost. There have been times in my life when, on the outside, I have been juggling more than ever, better than ever. But the behind-the-scenes cost is that I'm burnt-out, overwhelmed, self-critical and irritable.

- We never see the full picture unless people share it with us, and even then we see everything through our own lenses of understanding. The more we can be open with others, the more authentic conversations we can have, then the more confidence we will have in the sense that we aren't the only one with dark corners and rough edges!

- Recognize when you feel vulnerable to comparison. For me, I'm most vulnerable when I'm feeling exhausted as it takes energy to coach myself through those moments. Consider how you might place some boundaries that will help support you at these times. Perhaps you limit your social media use when tired, or you speak about your insecurities openly with a friend so that they can be the voice of balance and support you're looking for.

- Celebrate your strengths! We so often focus on what we feel we're lacking in, or we don't have, so it can be really beneficial to take a moment to be grateful for the things we have strength in, and do have!

- We can sometimes harness comparison as a motivating, driving factor to grow in a direction we would like to. I have a friend who seemed unfazed by the occasional disruptions in her baby's routine, whereas for me those situations provoked anxiety. I admired her, and rather then using this observation as a stick to beat myself up with for struggling with inflexibility, I asked her for encouragement and tips instead.

·········· **TIP:** ··········

When you notice you are comparing yourself
with someone else, gently ask yourself what
you're hoping for, or what you are looking
to feel validated in. How else might you
get what you need in the moment, either
from yourself or a trusted friend?

··········

See also:
Don't Feel Good Enough
Envious
Social Anxiety

crying

**It feels hard
because it
is hard**

baby

A crying baby can trigger feelings of helplessness and worry. Crying is designed to create a stress response in a mother's body so that we react and meet a need somehow, that's why your baby's cries feel amplified to you. But I know so well how tough it is if crying is prolonged, or you've just fallen into a desperately needed sleep.

As a mum of a reflux baby, I also know that crying can feel traumatic and how bonding can be hard when your baby doesn't seem to respond to your desperate attempts to meet their needs. I know the physical squirming feeling of helplessness that has driven me to tears as my baby has screamed in the car seat, hungry, when I've been stuck in traffic. It can feel physically and emotionally painful.

My crying baby would sometimes create this fight-or-flight-inducing thundercloud within me when my maternal instinct to love, comfort and protect collided with my human need for times of quiet and rest.

So whether you're having a rough day or trying to calm colic or reflux, here are my tips:

- If you have concerns that your baby is in pain, or crying levels are more than you think is 'normal', find a helpful doctor. If you feel misheard or overlooked, ask for a different doctor who might have special interest in infant colic or reflux.

- Find a way to get your space. I know it can be logistically tricky, and you can feel at war with your maternal heart as you step out alone for a loop round the block, but it doesn't mean you don't need it. You're not a bad mum for needing a breather, you're a human one.

- Seek *and accept* support. When you are exhausted and feel like your baby is unsettled, it can be hard to rationalize any feelings of failure. And when we are critical towards ourself, we can feel undeserving of the help or support we really need. Encourage yourself to seek support, whether it be a chat with your health visitor, the acceptance of an offer of a meal cooked by a friend, or a walk and a phone call to offload. You are deserving of support. Please, read that last sentence again out loud. Regardless of how you feel about yourself, seeking or accepting support is about keeping you okay. It's a self-esteem-boosting gesture of kindness to yourself.

- Don't be afraid to step away if you need to. There were times I'd have to step out of a room to do a round of breathing to calm my frayed nervous system and soften the fight-or-flight response. As long as your baby is safe, warm and fed, they will withstand a few moments of tears while you calm your precious heart, mind and body.

TIP:

Keeping on keeping on can feel like the only option when you're super independent. But ignoring your feelings and your human need for support will lead to burnout. If you are worried about yourself or your baby in any way, you deserve support, insight and input.

See also:
Baby Blues
Missing My Old Life
Winging It!

it
feels **ha**

because
it is **h**

rd

ard

depressed

**Depression isn't weakness.
It's a symptom of having
to be strong for too long**

In the depths of sleep deprivation and
postnatal depression after having my second
child, I remember I spoke to my mum. I told
her how everything felt so dark, like I was
walking through an underground tunnel,
plodding through, limping through, dragging

myself through in the hope that I might find the light at the end. Instead of feeling like I was getting closer to the heat of the sunshine, each day just seemed to fuel my fear that perhaps the tunnel would never end, and there would be no light.

She promised there would be light. I begged her to tell me when. When would it come? When would my laughter come from deep down within rather than forced insincerely from my throat? When would my smile cause the corners of my eyes to crease rather than make my cheeks ache with effort? When would my happiness no longer be a mask worn for the benefit of others but rise up and spill out from my heart?

The light came in time. First it found its way through small cracks in my tunnel as I let others support me. Then it grew in brightness as I found strength and started to value myself, my feelings and my needs. It kept coming as I pushed through guilt and fear in order to nourish, care for and respect myself. Now, I don't live life on a sunbeam, but the light and the dark, the highs and the lows, are more balanced for me. Often when I find myself edging towards depression, I use this as a red flag, a prompt to do a kind of inventory on my well-being. I ask these questions:

- How long have I been feeling like this?
- How am I treating myself in my thoughts? Has my internal dialogue become crueller and more critical rather than kind and compassionate?
- Am I prioritizing the actions and habits that help me or have they slipped?

- Am I talking openly enough to those who care about me?
- Am I taking opportunities to rest when they arise?
- What feelings might I have been overlooking or invalidating?
- What needs might I have been overlooking or invalidating?
- Have I been doing too much or too little?
- Who can I speak to about how I'm feeling? Do I need to speak with my doctor?
- Have I been doing the things that make me happy? Even in small ways?

When should I seek help?

My recommendation is that you are deserving of support regardless of how many boxes you might tick on a diagnostic checklist – your mental well-being is a huge priority. If you have sought out this page because you're asking yourself whether you're depressed, let this be enough to prompt you to reach out to someone you trust and also an appropriate professional. Your doctor will be able to make a note of how you're feeling, along with recommending relevant referrals or treatment plans.

Should I take medication if offered?

This is something you can speak to your doctor about. You may be able to book a double appointment in order to ask any questions you might have. While it wouldn't be ethical of me to make specific recommendations, I would always recommend that alongside any medication, you are also putting in place positive habits that support your needs and feelings and nurture self-esteem and confidence along the way.

I know it can feel hard and dark, exhausting, relentless and lonely. It might occasionally feel hopeless and this can be very scary (see Baby Blues on p. 14 for depression symptoms). But I can tell you this, just as my mum promised me, there will be light again, the sunshine will reappear. And the things that will help usher in that sunshine may take energy that you don't feel you have at the moment. But please, please, summon every little scrap of energy you have, scrape it from dark and dusty corners and use it to reach out and seek support. Just as your heart of hearts wishes your baby a life rich in happiness and hope, you (of equal value) deserve that too.

TIP:

Make one move today towards
seeking support, whether it's opening
up to someone you trust, or
booking an appointment.

See also:
Baby Blues
Suicidal
Tearful

don't
feel

**We were never meant to be enough
to fulfil the number of roles we do
to the standards we set ourselves**

good
enough

How many times do you question whether you are good enough? Whether you are doing a good enough job, being a good enough mum, partner, daughter, colleague, friend?

So many roles, so many standards to fulfil.

Have you ever thought that perhaps one of the reasons you don't feel good enough is – and this is going to sound a little bit controversial here – you're not good enough?

Perhaps the main reason you don't feel good enough is that you are one person. You were never created to fulfil all the roles you undertake in your life to the standards you are attempting to meet (set by yourself and others).

The 'not good enough' feeling fills the void between the mother you think you should be and the mother that you are. Think about that mother you think you should be. Is that do-able? Really? Like, really, really?

Do you know anyone who mothers in that way all the time? And when I say 'know', I don't mean glimpse the front-of-house, I mean know their behind-the-scenes. Because let me tell you, and I can do so with certainty having been a therapist for a decade, there is always a behind-the-scenes, there is always a cost.

'Good enough' has been steamrollered by perfectionism and comparison. Good enough is now substandard. We see snapshots of other people's mothering, and we merge them together into one supposedly attainable ideal of what it is to be a 'great mum'.

When you find yourself questioning whether you are enough, recognize where 'enough' has been replaced with 'perfect'.

Let's reclaim 'good enough' and see 'perfect' for what it is – an ever-moving goalpost, a dangled carrot, a mirage in the desert, a damaging fantasy.

And do you know what? When we embrace 'good enough' over perfectionism, we are teaching our children how to survive in an imperfect world that will inevitably fail and disappoint. Parenting is a long-haul job, it's a daily grind. We mother through sickness, highs and lows, sleep deprivation and fluctuating hormones. We need to have more grace for ourselves otherwise we will consistently be shaming ourselves for missing the impossible bar.

∽ **TIP:** ∽

When you find yourself aiming for perfect,
consider what you'd say to a friend. How
can you acknowledge your humanness
and your ever-changing emotional,
mental and physical resources?

See also:
Guilty
Overwhelmed
Who Am I?

envious

**Feeling envious isn't
being a bad mother,
it's being a human one**

We want to be nice people, nice mums,
friendly, likeable, loving. So when the green-
eyed monster rears its head, you can
immediately catapult to judging yourself. To
accept yourself isn't to filter your human
feelings and only approve of the 'nice' ones.
Feeling the whole spectrum of emotion isn't

being a 'bad' person or mother, that's simply being a human one.

Nobody is immune to envy, it's what we do with it that makes the difference. You can't control what feelings come, but you can decide what you do with them. Left unchecked, envy can drive a wedge between friends and family, it can leave you feeling less-than and critical of yourself.

So, when you feel a stab of envy, what can you do with it? Here are three steps.

1 **Acknowledge** Accepting something doesn't mean you're going to leave it as it is! It just means that you accept that it's a feeling you're having right now. Acknowledging something and naming it means you can respond to it constructively rather than react on autopilot.

2 **Investigate** Consider what might be
behind the envy. Is it because you feel
lacking in some way? Is it perhaps a sense
of loss or grief that someone has something
you lost, or your heart so wishes you had?
Might it be that you are making
assumptions, for example if the mum at
the playgroup looks happy and well put
together, then she truly is? When you open
up envy, you often discover feelings of not
being good enough, hurt, loss, fear or
sadness.

3 **Respond** Respond kindly to envy. Self-
criticism gets us nowhere, but
self-compassion enables us to acknowledge
and move through an emotion rather than
feel stifled and stuck in it. You're not a bad
person for feeling envious. How might you
help yourself in this moment? Perhaps this

envy can move you to work on your self-esteem, or have a conversation with a friend about the envy you feel about this aspect of their lives. When we talk about envy in an honest way, it can be like disarming a bomb before it detonates. 'To be honest, I find myself so envious of your happy relationship when all me and my partner are doing is sniping at each other.' Perhaps you can acknowledge that your envy is a result of seeing someone excel in an area where you desire to see growth. Maybe it can be a launch pad to addressing procrastination or unhelpful habits so that you too can grow in this area!

·········· **TIP:** ··········

Note down in your journal the different kinds of envy you have felt recently. Go through the three steps and see how the feeling changes.

··········

See also:
Comparing Myself
Don't Feel Good Enough
Social Anxiety

exhausted

**I am deserving of rest
and slowing down**

Let any guilt that you're not functioning as quickly, efficiently or to the standard you'd like to, fall away. You're exhausted because it's exhausting, not because you don't have enough capacity, or because you need to be 'more' of anything. In an ideal world, a few nights of uninterrupted sleep would do the world of good but, realistically, how likely is that

61

right now? As much as I'd like to gift you some good, deep, nourishing sleep, I'm going to give you some other ways to get some rest so that you can refuel along the way.

First of all, I just quickly want to say a couple of things about rest. Our culture seems to have got it all upside down over the years. As humans we are created to live *from* a place of rest, whereas these days we seem to work towards a place of collapse, believing we need to earn our way to rest, and often even then feeling guilty when we slow down.

Contrary to belief and where it gets placed in our diaries, Sunday used to be the start of the week, the day of rest (remember when the shops were shut on Sundays?). Because that's how we work most efficiently, when we start from rest. Our culture now lives to the beat of the drum that pounds 'you are what you do, what you earn, what you have and how efficient you are'. We tend to drive ourselves to a place of exhaustion, believing we can only enjoy rest when we have ticked off everything on the to-do list. The thing is, the to-do list never ends and we become more exhausted, burnt-out and unwell than ever.

So, how can you change this for yourself as you mother? How can you teach yourself and your child the countercultural message that you are deserving of rest, and that the sum of your worth is not what and how much you do? That's what I want to teach my children! I want them to know that they are more than their achievements, their material possessions or their efficiency, therefore I must model it for them (which is tough when the message is so deeply engrained, but sure is possible).

Say this out loud: **'I deserve rest. I deserve to slow down. I am not the sum of what I do.'**

The more you give, the more you need. It's a simple science that we don't question when we drive our car! The more miles you go, the more fuel you need, and the same goes for you. Plus, you fuel the car at the start of the journey, not at the end! Rest is both a recovery from the challenging moments and a way to save up some fuel for the ones to come. Rest is not selfish; it is a building block for good mental and physical well-being. It's also brilliant for relationships! I am a much nicer person to be around when I am not my burnt-out, irritable, irrational, rest-refusing self. Rest isn't only vital, it's actually an act of love for those around you!

Now, I know rest is hard to come by, so here are some ways to refuel:

- Don't overlook any chance to rest, regardless of how small it is. If you were dehydrated in the desert and you came across the smallest pool of water, would you think, 'There's no point stopping and drinking that. I need so much more than that tiny puddle'? No, you'd slurp it up, every drop, so that you could continue on. If you have five minutes to sit down, take it. If you have a chance for a quick phone call with an old friend, take it. It's not what it is so much as what it gives you.

- Be more single-minded. Us mothers are masters of multitasking! We head upstairs to grab a nappy and do another nine jobs along the way. While efficient, it also uses energy you don't have at the moment. Every time we gear shift (think cooking

65

dinner while answering an email, tidying a drawer, firing off a text message) it is a micro stressor as our attention constantly shifts and hops everywhere. For now, try to simplify things so that you can focus on the task at hand and let your brain rest when it can.

- When you find yourself saying 'I just need to . . .', ask yourself: 'Do I? Can it wait? Can I delegate it to another person or another day when I've got more energy?'

- Consider what boundaries you might be able to place around your diary, your phone or the things you say yes to at this time. I no longer go on my email or social media between 9 p.m. and 9 a.m. and I can say it has actually changed my life!

- When you find yourself saying 'I can't rest', instead say 'I'm not prioritizing rest for myself right now.' It adds an element of decision-making into it, and welcomes the possibility that perhaps you can prioritize yourself more than you might usually do so.

- Shun perfectionism and cut corners. Doing everything brilliantly and from scratch takes energy you don't necessarily need to be spending right now. There will be energy for that another day, but right now you need to reserve what you can.

- Pause before you say yes to invitations. Say 'Let me check my diary' and take a moment to think about the level of your energy and resources, and the wider picture of what you're doing that week that might take from you physically, emotionally or socially. Sometimes when you say yes to someone else, you're saying no to meeting your own fundamental needs.

- Do things slower. Literally, slow the pace of what you do and think, if you can. Leave extra time so that you can avoid rushing your way through the day.

- Take a moment to close your eyes. It might not be the hours of sleep you're craving, but it provides a little bit of sensory deprivation to calm your nervous system.

Often these things don't feel enough, but they're something. And something is always better than nothing. A small breather or boundary placed might just be enough to top you up for the next challenge that arises.

TIP:

Don't pass up an opportunity to do something restful. In fact, seek them out each day. Ride any waves of guilt and know that the more you give, the more you need.

See also:
Insomnia
Overwhelmed
Tearful

I am
deserving

of rest and

slowing

down

feel like a

**Sharing the burden
doesn't turn you
into one**

burden

Oh, the familiar feeling that arises when someone offers to help, does something kind, or asks if I'm okay, and sounds like they want to hear more than my autopilot response. The worry that in accepting their offer or gesture, no matter how well-meaning, I'm indebted to them and my cascade of 'thank you's won't suffice. The concern that I will be a burden, that they are quietly hoping I'll decline so they can breathe a secret sigh of relief. The fear that spending their time, energy or resources on me will leave them feeling overwhelmed or resentful.

It's not only grand gestures that have had me feeling this fear, but even the simplest ones. The phone calls to see how I am, the thoughtful birthday gift, the making me a cup of tea in my home because I'm pinned down by a sleeping baby. Because of this fear, I've turned down help when I've needed it most, allowing myself to slip further into lonely exhaustion.

Challenging the fear of being a burden has categorically changed my life and my relationships. Because you know what? I have willingly and lovingly helped carry the little and large burdens of other people in my life because I've wanted to help and support them. And who am I to say that I am not worthy of others standing beside me too? Getting better at accepting support and acts of kindness has been and continues to be a journey for me, but it's such a vital one as I seek to teach my children that they, too, are worthy of asking for and accepting love and support through the rough and the smooth, the twists and the turns.

Here are some things that help me when I fear being a burden:

- Challenge yourself to say 'thank you' and 'yes please' even when everything inside of you wants to say 'I'm fine, thanks, don't worry'. Feel the fear and say yes anyway. In time, you may find yourself growing in confidence.

- Think about when you help others, how does it feel? Does it feel like an honour? It's nice to afford others that same privilege of the warm feeling that comes with supporting someone and knowing you've made a difference somehow.

- Remind yourself that friendship ebbs and flows. Sometimes one person needs more support than the other, but then things switch round again! Being the supporter might feel more comfortable for you, but this is the nature of friendship, and this is *your* time!

- If you, like me, have found it hard to have boundaries around how you spend your time and energy on people, it can lead to overwhelm, exhaustion and feelings of resentment. You may assume that others will feel overwhelmed, exhausted and resentful after supporting you.
- Feelings aren't facts. Feeling like a burden doesn't mean you are one!
- You may have supported someone else through a challenging time and it felt hard or sacrificial. But sometimes we do sacrifice our energy or resources for those we love, because it's important to us. Someone going out of their way to help you is an act of love and support.
- You can only be responsible for how authentic your own offers of support are. You cannot control where someone else places their boundaries, or if they choose

to offer support that isn't coming from an authentic place. We are all responsible for placing our own boundaries around our energy and resources.

- If possible, share your fear of being a burden with that person. Maybe they can offer you some words of reassurance.

Right now, at this time in your life, you need and deserve more support and care than ever as you juggle and navigate early motherhood through tired eyes. Leaning on others isn't failure or weakness, but a vital human necessity. The more comfortable you can become in accepting the smaller gestures of support, the more able you will be to ask for it and accept it when you need it most of all.

TIP:

Challenge yourself to say yes to offers
of help and support, and then ride
the wave of guilt or fear of being a
burden rather than letting it stop
you receiving something you need.

See also:

Guilty
Lonely
Resentful

grateful

**Gratitude welcomes
joy into my moments**

It's such a good feeling, isn't it, to feel that
warmth of gratitude? Where do you feel it in
your body? What other emotions roll in as you
focus on what you are feeling grateful for? For
this moment, this very one you are in now as
you are reading these words and feeling that
warmth, is the only thing in life that truly exists.
This is where you are, this is where the living is.
Embrace it, take a moment to add detail to the

story of your gratitude. If your baby inspired gratitude, think about what you love about them – the texture of their skin, the tone of their laughter. Let the gratitude swell like a building wave.

What I love about gratitude is that it turns our attention from what is hard, and what we'd like to change, towards what is good and right and real, and what we are enjoying in the moment. It's not a denial that other things are happening in our lives which are challenging, but it's welcoming in the *and*. Things are challenging *and* wonderful, at the same time.

We often refer to life as a roller coaster of twists and turns, of ups and downs. But gratitude encourages us to see life more like a train track, where the wild and the wonderful exist beside one another, winding and weaving together.

I love this idea, that no matter how rough the ride may feel, there is always something that will bring us this beautiful, warm, honey-sweet sense of gratitude. And for me, gratitude brings joy, it adds a spring in my step, it turns a light on in what may otherwise feel like a grey room. It's always there for the taking, even if sometimes it can feel like we have to be really intentional in seeking it.

I will never forget the moment my washing machine made me cry. I was huffing and puffing, focused on the relentlessness of washing in our household, how it comes thick and fast with little let-up, as I shoved the pants and shirts into the drum. The mundane sure can feel exhausting! I decided to welcome some gratitude, listing all the things I felt grateful for in that moment. I felt grateful for the machine itself, the water we have access to, the house that keeps us safe, the fact that we have clothes that fit to keep us warm. I felt grateful for my hands that deftly moved the stray socks out of the basket, and for the family who had worn them who make my life so full. All of these things are, in themselves, immense privileges that I so often take for granted. And as I added to my list, I felt my heart lift and my eyes tear. The job was still mundane, but I had seen the beauty around it. Mundane *and* beautiful.

So welcome and enjoy this feeling. And it's there for the taking even on the darkest and most difficult of days . . . if you look hard enough. Gratitude need not invalidate your feelings of overwhelm, exhaustion or sadness, but it can usher in others to sit beside them.

TIP:

When feeling frustrated or bogged down in the mundanity of life, turn 'I've got to' into 'I get to'. For example 'I've got to do the night feed' turns into 'I'm exhausted and I get to cuddle my baby in the quiet night, just me and them together.'

See also:
Comparing Myself
Self-care
Winging It!

grieving

Grief is no reflection on how much you love what you have

It's the aching feeling in your heart that has no other balm but time. It feels heavy as it rolls over you like a wave, peaking and subsiding, bringing with it tears or an echoing emptiness.

I always used to think that we only grieved death, the loss of a person we loved. And we do, deeply. But I have learned over the years that we grieve for more than people. We grieve many things. We grieve the loss of what has been before, we grieve the predictable and comfortable that has been nudged aside for new and uncharted territory. We can grieve the loss of things, a precious item of jewellery mislaid on a sandy beach or down a plug hole. We grieve our hopes and dreams, the realization that what we had yearned for looks different in the flesh of the day-to-day mundane.

As a new mum, amongst the elation, the joy, the love and adoration, I have felt many griefs. Here are some you may identify with:

- **The loss of pre-baby life** Life has changed immeasurably, and it's not a bad thing, of course! But with it, little looks the same, not your diary nor your day-to-day life, not to mention your feelings, your hormones, the sudden growth in the capacity of your heart to love.

   As humans, we thrive on predictability and routine. For many of us, those have been the lifeboats that kept us feeling safe and secure. So to grieve for your old normal where you had a freedom to meet your needs, a greater sense of control in dictating what you did and when, isn't a resentment for what you have now! Let me say that again as it's so important – this grief isn't a resentment of your baby, it's an acknowledgement of the shifts and changes. We can grieve what has been before, when all feels at sea and new. That grief isn't saying that what is new isn't good, it's just different!

- **The loss of a dream** As I sat with stretched, shiny breasts upon the hormonal roller coaster of the post-birth days, as I mopped up vomit and tried to blink away the scratchy feeling of tired eyes, I thought how different the reality was to the fantasy of motherhood I had had in my mind. As I let go of the perfect dream that had been fuelled by social media and fairy tales, I felt a sadness. Motherhood was grittier and so much more physically and mentally challenging than I had imagined. However, it was also far richer than my daydreams could ever have conjured up. I never knew that I would be challenged and transformed in the most incredible ways as I walked through those early days, months and years. I'd take the Technicolor, gritty reality over my 2D fantasy any day, but still, it was a loss of sorts as I let the candyfloss, baby-powder-scented dreams float away.

- **The loss of what could have been**
  As we focus on what we *do* have, our mind often turns to what could have been. New life can prompt us to reflect on what we have lost. Perhaps you have lost a loved one, or endured a miscarriage or baby loss, and find yourself feeling a sadness as

you think of the milestones that haven't
been shared, or how the family
photographs are missing that familiar
face. Joy for what you have and sadness
for what could have been can reside side
by side, neither one making a statement
about the validity of the other.

When it comes to feeling those waves of grief,
the most important thing I want you to take from
this section is to be gentle towards yourself.
I have felt ashamed for feeling grief at what was,
or what could have been. I have tried to shut
down those feelings out of fear and self-
judgement. For how can I feel grief when I love
my new baby? How dare I reflect on what was,
when what I have is so much more valuable to
me? We need gentleness, because we are simply
processing and recognizing the complexity of a
huge shift in life. We have to remind ourselves

that conflicting feelings in motherhood are so very normal, and so very human. We can feel both love and sadness in one, neither of them dictating the validity of the other.

· · · · · · · · · · **TIP:** · · · · · · · · · ·

Ride those waves of grief, acknowledge them respectfully and let them roll over you. If you feel overwhelmed or confused, please do seek support (see the Helpful Contacts section at the end of this book) as sometimes it makes the world of difference to have someone supporting us as we navigate how closely love and loss collide.

· · · · · · · · · ·

See also:
Baby Blues
Missing My Old Life
Tearful

conflicting
feelings in
mother

and so very
human

hood

are so very

normal,

guilty

**Guilt is there
to prompt you,
not to shame you**

Guilt can easily become the background buzz
to motherhood. Guilt about not doing enough,
well enough, efficiently enough . . . guilt for
resting, for needing space, for feeling
overwhelmed. Guilt for accepting support, for
finding things challenging, for not loving every

moment. The opportunities for guilt are limitless!

Guilt sits like a heavy black rock in your stomach, causing the volume of your inner critic to soar and your self-esteem to plummet. Holding on to guilt is a form of self-bullying! Guilt is best seen as a little red flag that pops up to prompt you, and not as a reason to criticize yourself.

Next time you feel guilty, don't just let it sit there making you feel like a bad mum, use my three step 'ACT' approach:

Address

A Address the guilt by naming the reason you feel guilty. Imagine taking that black rock of guilt out of your stomach and placing it on your open palm. 'I feel guilty because . . .'

Compassion

C Now, you are deserving of compassion. That's a fact! Regardless of what you feel about yourself, you are worthy of kindness.

How can you be compassionate towards that feeling of guilt? Remind yourself: 'You're exhausted, you meant well, things were stressful, you're human!'

Perhaps you can acknowledge with compassion that the guilt you feel isn't actually justified. If so, tell yourself that what you feel guilty about isn't actually about 'fault' at all. I felt such guilt about the unhappiness of my refluxy baby. That wasn't my guilt to carry, I hadn't actually done anything wrong!

If you find this hard, imagine how you'd respond to a friend struggling with the same thing. Often, it's easier to find compassion for someone you care about, so turn some of that towards yourself.

Tweak

Finally, if the guilt were to prompt you to do something, what might that be? Maybe it is simply there to encourage you to seek support, insight or techniques to help you approach the situation differently next time. Maybe it's a prompt to weave some slowness into your day because you are overwhelmed and irritability is coming out sideways. Might you need to open up to a friend to help you process some of these feelings and bring some welcome balance and compassion into them?

Once you have gone through the ACT steps, decide to let that guilt go (even if it keeps repeating on you!). You've let it prompt you, and it has done its job.

☀
TIP:

Spend some time jotting down the
different kinds of guilt you have been
carrying, and then go through my ACT
process in writing. You can return to this
when you next find yourself picking up
that heavy black rock again!

See also:
Information Overload
Judged
Self-care

hormonal

**I wonder if my feelings
are a nod to the needs
I normally overlook?**

How are you feeling in this moment? Hormones
are responsible for regulating so many systems
in your body, from growth to metabolism, from
mood to body temperature. Having a baby is
a huge hormonal event, so it's utterly
understandable that the powerful hormonal
systems that have helped you grow your baby
are taking you on a roller coaster along with
them, as they take a while to settle back down
into a rhythm.

Take a moment to do some grounding breaths right now. Breathe in for six counts and steadily out for eight. Try to complete ten rounds if you're able to.

Hormones are powerful things, so whether you're feeling irritable, overwhelmed, sensitive to noise or sensation, low, sluggish or angry, you're not broken, you're normal.

This is quite a different take on how you're feeling right now. What I did for many years was to just dismiss my feelings as 'hormonal'. While hormones can often explain the intensity of emotion, this doesn't mean that you need to invalidate what you're feeling or write it off as irrational. When we are exhausted or feeling depleted by hormones (or anything else for that matter), we tend to be less defended against our emotions. Pushing our emotions down or spending a moment to make sense of them both take time and energy. So I encourage you to consider . . . what if you are just seeing more clearly what lies beneath your usual facade? What if your sudden need for space or quiet, or that swelling feeling of resentment, isn't just 'hormones' but a nod to a need that you might be ignoring when your hormones aren't playing such a part? Note these feelings, tend to them, try to observe them rather than write them off or shove them aside.

The more we respect our emotions and find ways to acknowledge them rather than push them down, the less likely they are to come out sideways. For example, when I can acknowledge that I'm feeling sensitive, I'm less likely to pick a fight with my partner over something that may not bother me in a few days. Perhaps I'd even say to him that I was feeling particularly emotional or sensitive so that he could be extra gentle. The more I respect my exhaustion, the more likely I am to find a way to get rest or to knock something off my to-do list for another day.

I'm not going to give you an in-depth science lesson on hormones but it is undeniable that there are some major hormonal shifts that occur in the weeks and months after giving birth. I would really encourage you to have a read and do some research on how your hormones shift and change over the post-partum period, because it can help offer insight into why you may be feeling the way you are.

I don't know about you, but I feel a sharp increase in irritability and tearfulness before my period, and when I haven't connected the dots that my period is about to arrive, I tend to lean towards being frustrated and annoyed at myself for feeling so irrational. However, when I look at my app (I use an app to track my cycle), it suddenly makes sense. When I can clearly see the cyclical, rhythmic nature of this feeling, I can remind myself and reassure myself that the cloud will pass as it always does. Also, I can find self-compassion in place of some of the criticism, and maybe even find ways to make the road a little smoother for myself by lowering expectations and letting others know how I'm feeling so that they can bring some of the grounding and rationality I need.

So, if you don't track your cycle, it can be a really useful thing to begin to do, to help predict and navigate the patterns of the monthly hormone flux. Note down feelings and mood so that as things settle into a cycle, you can look back and see if you felt the same way previously. If you feel low or question whether you might be experiencing more hormonal imbalance than you were expecting to at this point, please do speak to your doctor so that they can explore things further if necessary.

TIP:

Think about how you can simplify things for yourself right now. Is there some pressure you can remove from yourself? An opportunity for rest, a hug, some encouragement or support you can take someone up on? How can you make the road smoother for yourself as you navigate this hormonal feeling?

———

See also:
Baby Blues
Exhausted
Tearful

information

**Your intuition is
a powerful tool**

overload

Gone are the days when the first advice or input sought was from inside ourself, from our own intuition, that little sense of peace or unease deep down in our core that tells us whether something is okay or worth worrying about. Gone are the days when the first port of call was to speak to a friend or family member to affirm what we sensed was right.

Instead, we are flooded with information, advice and opinion everywhere we turn, whether we're asking for it or not. Back in the day, if we wanted to learn about what was going on in the news, we'd pick up a paper or switch on the TV at a certain time. If we had a worry about our child, we'd speak to a friend or an experienced family member. If we had a health concern, we'd make an appointment with the doctor. These days we are bombarded with avenues of information. Health concern? Scroll through reams of contradictory online articles, leaving yourself more confused and worried than before.

We humans are perceptive; we can find strength we didn't know we had in moments that blindside us. But our powerful intuition can get silenced by the roaring noise of information around us. It can also get distorted by unaddressed anxieties and fears.

Sure, knowledge can be power, but it can become destructive and confusing when we're overwhelmed by it.

Here's how to tap back into your motherhood intuition next time you hit a challenge or decision:

- Stop for a moment. Breathe. Ask yourself what you *feel* is right. What sits best with you, even if on paper it doesn't look quite right?

- Address your anxieties. Anxiety and overthinking can distort our intuition because we are viewing our situation through the lens of fear. Find tools and techniques to address the anxieties that arise in day-to-day life, so that your intuition will feel less clouded by fear.
- Try some free writing in your journal. Just write whatever comes to mind, even if it doesn't make sense. It can be so interesting to see what is revealed when we let our minds and feelings have space.
- Limit how often you access news and information. It's such a cultural habit to reach for the internet when we have a question or decision to make, but it can actually end up bringing more confusion

and contradiction rather than the clarity you were hungering for.

- Commit to consulting yourself first, then someone trusted, and then another information source if necessary (preferably a reputable or professional source rather than a subjective opinion).

- Seek advice from those who will let you talk things through rather than jump to fix it with their own advice or opinion. Sometimes I ask friends whether they can be a sounding board for me to talk something through. Often when we verbalize things we end up finding more confidence in our own conclusions.

- Remind yourself that your way won't be everyone's way. What feels right for you and your baby may look different for someone else. Different doesn't equal wrong.

TIP:

Note down the moments in your
life where you followed your intuition
and it worked out well. This can be a
powerful reinforcer of how wonderfully
intuitive you naturally are!

See also:
Anxious
Panicking
Unsolicited Advice

insomnia

**All forms of rest are
beneficial to me**

If you've ever wanted to deftly poke someone
who said 'sleep when the baby sleeps' as they've
gazed at your eye bags, then this is for you. How
can you be so darned exhausted and yet, when
given the opportunity to sleep, you just can't?

Sleep deprivation can be absolutely
excruciating. I'm writing as someone who often

had forty-five minutes a night sleep with an undiagnosed refluxy baby. Having a rough night has such an impact on how you feel the next day, how well you can rationalize thoughts and feelings, and navigate decisions. But with a baby who wakes unpredictably, the last thing you need is the frustration of not being able to sleep when you can.

Here are some reasons you might be finding it hard:

- **Feelings rise up** You have just undergone a huge life shift in having a baby. That is a lot to process, and if you're a 'thinker' or a 'worrier' it might be that, as you lie down and switch off the light, all of those concerns and feelings that have been hovering under the surface rear their heads for attention!

What to do Note and acknowledge feelings and fears as they arise in the day. Try keeping a journal next to your bed and jotting them down. Use some grounding techniques as you cosy up, such as counting back from 100 in threes to disrupt the thoughts, or breathing in for four counts and out for six to calm any adrenaline and stress response in your body.

- **The hormone roller coaster** There are so many hormonal changes that occur when you've had a baby. Progesterone decreases, affecting the levels of melatonin, which is your sleepy hormone.

   What to do Go for a walk each day. Even if you're exhausted, this exposure to daylight will help balance your circadian rhythm. Monitor caffeine, sugar and alcohol intake, all of which can impact the sleep rhythms of your body.

- **Not enough rest** The washing pile is building by the moment, the post has stacked up and the vacuum cleaner is staring at you. By keeping on the go all the time and ignoring your need to slow down, your body is likely to feel that mixture of tired and wired. So when the opportunities do arise to slow down or sleep, everything is too revved up to relax into rest.

  What to do You need to reprioritize rest. Do things slower, cut corners, take it easier on yourself, reprioritizing your needs over the needs of the house. If you are prioritizing the state of your home over your basic needs, then you're giving yourself the message that your needs are less important than a washing pile. Those things will get done more efficiently if you are refuelled. Restful things such as sitting down to read or closing your eyes for a moment might not be the sleep you are craving, but they are beneficial.

- **You get frustrated at being awake**
  I can literally feel my stress level rise in the moments I gaze at my sleeping baby while I lie restless. It's incredibly frustrating, yet the adrenaline pushes the likelihood of sleep further away.

  What to do Calm your body and mind using the breathing and distraction tips on p. 112. Repeat to yourself 'All rest is beneficial' as a reminder that you're benefiting from being still and comfortable. I also found it helpful to know that the first stage of sleep feels wakeful (you know, when your thoughts are all awry and a bit surreal?), so sometimes I may be more asleep than I believe!

·········· **TIP:** ··········

Speak with your healthcare practitioner if you'd like some advice, if you're feeling low, or if your hormones feel particularly out of kilter.

··········

See also:

Exhausted
Intrusive Thoughts
Tearful

all forms of
rest

are
beneficial
to me

intrusive

**My intrusive thoughts
aren't a reflection of
who I am**

thoughts

Intrusive thoughts are those horrible thoughts that thrust themselves into your mind. I get them all the time and used to be afraid of them. I thought that perhaps they were premonitions, or that I must be a terrible person for imagining such things! I'd see visions of pile-ups on the motorway that had me sweating at the next service station, or I'd imagine myself pushing over a table of pyramid-stacked mugs in a gift shop. Intrusive thoughts come under many guises and can easily have you questioning your personality and your sanity.

We give intrusive thoughts so much power, yet they deserve none. For they are just thoughts.

Intrusive thoughts are fear-based thoughts in which your mind rifles through many scenarios in a single second. Your brain is always assessing risk, responsibility, power and choice as you go about life, and these intrusive thoughts can be the result.

My mind would see my buggy roll towards the busy road, prompting me to put the brake on as I stood talking to a friend. My fear of something bad happening to my precious baby would weave my mind's simple warning into a heart-shattering tale that I'd keep replaying every time I walked too close to the pavement's edge.

Another hugely common intrusive thought for mums plays out around stairs. Visions of dropping or throwing my baby down the stairs would plague me, having me questioning my worthiness to be a mother. It felt like a shameful secret, but the more I understood intrusive thoughts, the less power they held over me. I hope this helps you too.

Some tips for the next time you get an intrusive thought:

- Starve the thought of attention by imagining it as a mouldy old leaf that has passed you in the breeze. Blow it on by with a big exhale of breath. Try to avoid the temptation to grab it and study it.
- This thought has probably seized your attention because it is so wildly out of line with you and your morals, or it has echoes of your fears or traumas. Remind yourself that it is just a thought, it is not you.
- If you have begun to ruminate over the thought, count back from 100 in threes to deter your brain from thinking further.
- If you're feeling anxious, calm your nervous system by practising a breathing exercise. Inhale deeply for four counts, exhale for six. Do this ten times or until

you feel your heart rate slow and your shoulders drop.

- Remind yourself that while the thought itself may be shocking, it's not a prediction of your future, it is just your creative brain thinking up scenarios.
- Imagine the mundane, most likely alternative scenario. If my intrusive thought is that something bad will happen overnight, I imagine waking up to the noises of my hungry baby.
- If your intrusive thoughts feel relentless or traumatic, please consider engaging in therapy or counselling as you are deserving of support in disempowering them.

TIP:

When you are tired, hormonal or under stress (for example, experiencing the massive life-shifting event of having a baby enter your world), you have less of the energy needed to rationalize and halt rumination on these intrusive thoughts. So treat yourself with kindness and compassion as you navigate the thoughts that come your way, and speak to a trusted friend if possible so that they can offer some grounding support.

See also:
Anxious
Depressed
Insomnia

irritable

**If irritability was a
sign of unmet needs,
what might those
needs be for me?**

I don't like being irritable. It's like the worst of
myself pops out at any given opportunity and it's
hard to rein in. My words come out sharper than
I mean them to and I feel less able to rationalize
and bring balance to what's going on around me.
Things I might normally be able to brush off

suddenly feel intolerable. Emotions I might usually contain or calm with compassion instead spill over and create a mess that I later have to clean up somehow, with an apology or an explanation.

The less energy you have, the less your resources are topped up through rest, connection and self-care, the less you are able to process emotions and feelings constructively in the way that you would like to.

Here are three 'what' questions to ask yourself when you feel irritable:

1   **What is making me irritable?** I don't mean the dripping tap, the washing pile or the confusingly worded text from a friend, I mean what is missing that might usually enable you to navigate this in the way that you would like to?

Maybe sleep is missing or perhaps your normal hormonal rhythm. Maybe it's support, understanding. Or it might be those little things you did pre-baby that nourished you somehow – carefree laughter with friends, space to do your thing, your old exercise routine that used to give you a high.

2 **What is missing from my resources?** Now this is the tricky bit because often what you want isn't something you can have! Or it requires more logistics than you have energy to organize. You might want a full night's sleep, a holiday, or for colic to *adios* itself out of the door.

So then look at the underlying need beyond that:

A full night's sleep = rest

A holiday = change of context

Colic to *adios* out of the door = relief for my baby and a break from the stress.

3 What can I do to meet my needs?

How might you meet those needs, even if it's in a small way that tops up your resources a smidge?

Rest = put aside the washing

Change of context = drive to a new place for the afternoon

Relief for my baby and a break from the stress = research some colic relief tips and take a baby-free walk for half an hour while listening to a podcast.

⟨ — **TIP:** — ⟩

In your journal, scribble down
answers to the three 'what' questions
and then find a way to act on at
least one of those needs today.

———

See also:
Overwhelmed
Resentful
Self-care

judged

**Judgement
is opinion, not fact**

I don't know about you, but when I feel
misunderstood it taps into all those feelings of
worrying that I'm not good enough. I can go
from feeling completely fine to feeling ashamed
and questioning myself. What happens in your
body and mind when you feel judged? What
sensations rise up and what do you feel
prompted to do? Perhaps you want to explain
or defend yourself.

Here are my tips for those moments when you
feel judged.

- **If you feel judged by someone, ask yourself, 'Is this a true fact or is it an opinion?'** When we judge each other, we are normally making a personal assessment of a very small part of what we see. We may not know the full picture or story, and our opinion is formed by our own unique world view. Therefore, consider how valid that judgement is.

- **Know that feeling judged and being judged are two different things** Often the things I feel judged about are those areas in which I already feel a bit insecure or uncertain. If someone looks at me in a certain way when I have a crying baby in a supermarket and I already feel stressed and worried, I might assume they are thinking negatively of me. The assumptions we make are powerful and can drive us deeper into that feeling of shame and not being good enough. In these moments, I remind myself: 'They might be judging me or they might not' – this helps shake up that feeling of certainty!

- **Anchor yourself in what you know to be true** Consider what you know to be true about the situation and ground yourself in the facts. Let's say you feel judged because you approach routine differently to a friend. What are the facts here? A) You are doing what you feel works best for you and your child. B) There are many different ways to approach things. C) 'Different' doesn't need to equal 'wrong'. D) You love your child and want them to thrive.

- **Become acquainted with being misunderstood** If feeling misunderstood is a bit of a trigger and finds you desperate to 'put it right', it can be life-changing to become slowly comfortable with it. When you feel judged by someone who has only seen a small part of your bigger picture, imagine blowing it away like a fluffy cloud and hold on to those sturdy, iron anchors of fact. It takes a lot of energy to change the opinion of someone who might only be judging others negatively to bring themselves a sense of confidence in their own decisions and approaches. You need that energy for other things!

- **Start a conversation** If you feel judged by someone you know well and it is negatively impacting your relationship or friendship, how might you talk to them? In talking you may gain clarity on what they are thinking, instead of what you *think* they are thinking. Also, sometimes people aren't even aware of how or why they are judging someone, or that it is impacting the relationship. One would hope that a healthy, mutually caring relationship would be able to withstand differing opinions and decisions, or an honest, open and respectful discussion about them.

TIP:

Be gentle with yourself when you are feeling judged. There is a little version of ourselves inside all of us who just wants to feel loved, affirmed and understood. When we do not feel those things, we can grow in confidence by coaching ourselves gently through such moments.

See also:
Comparing Myself
Information Overload
Unsolicited Advice

lonely

I am not alone in feeling lonely

You are not alone in feeling lonely. It can seem like the world closes in when you have a baby. I felt like my life went from moving in many circles and contexts to being stuck in the confines of the sofa, the bedroom and the walk to my local town. How come even though I was never alone, I was often lonely?

134

I want to offer you some reasons for this feeling of loneliness you are experiencing. Not because I want to troubleshoot or fix it, but I want to help ease some of the guilt that often comes with loneliness in motherhood. Do your feelings of loneliness come with guilt like mine did? I felt guilt that the happiness of motherhood wasn't enough to quench the sense of being lonely, as if somehow I wasn't appreciative enough of the privilege of having a baby, or I wasn't doing enough to nurture my friendships.

Here are some reasons you may be feeling lonely, despite not being physically alone:

- You are spending most of your time with your baby. Your baby, although wonderful and valued, cannot fulfil all your needs for social interaction, love and connection.

- This postnatal time is intense and often takes you physically away from other people. The hours I sat in a dark room with an overtired baby or shushing and rocking in a quiet spot away from family meant that at times it felt life was happening and memories were being made without me.

- Relationships go through transitions when you have a baby. Old friendships shift and new friendships feel, well, sometimes too new to bare all and open up about the heights and depths. We can feel misunderstood by those struggling to navigate this new version of us.

- The days can feel long and limited when dictated by feeds and naps, and life has shifted from a routine of work and socializing to being more home-based.

- Physical tiredness and birth recovery can make socializing feel like an arduous task

and getting out of the house seem like an
expedition that sometimes you just don't
have the energy for.

- It can be a challenge to get quality time
with those you love and care about, those
who you can completely be yourself
around.
- Baby groups can feel daunting when you
are low on social energy or suffer from
social anxiety walking into a new group of
people.

Acknowledging all these reasons can help to
strip the nagging guilt away from loneliness. It's
so easy to tell ourselves that we 'should' be
feeling a certain way, but the circumstances of
this post-partum time make loneliness a very
common experience. So you're not failing,
you're just having a normal, human response to
your circumstances.

However, let me bring some hope and some encouragement. This feeling of loneliness will shift and change as life opens up for you again beyond the sofa and these days that feel lived on repeat. In the meantime, here are some things that will help:

- Mix up your days in small and comfortable ways. Pledge to step outside each day. Perhaps you walk a different route to town or do one of baby's naps in the buggy while out and about in the fresh air.
- Seek connection with at least one person you know per day. Whether it's a new friend or an old one, a phone call or a visit to share coffee on the sofa, a quick catch-up or a deep and meaningful one, try to commit to connecting with another adult each day.
- I feel that loneliness is a type of disconnection from the world. If the

opposite to disconnection is connection, then vulnerability and openness are balms for loneliness. Do you have someone you can be honest with about how you're feeling? They might not be able to 'fix' it for you, but having your feelings heard and comforted is so important.

- When you're alone, how might you feel a bit more comfortable in your own company? Recognize your inner dialogue. If it's sounding a little more critical than kind, try to introduce a more compassionate voice. It's easier to spend time with yourself when the conversations you have with yourself throughout the day are more supportive than critical.

- Think about the things that usually bring you joy and make you smile. Which of those things can you introduce into your day? It might be a funny box set you used to love, or a creative project you keep on the table to engage in when you feel able.

- Lean on others. Practise saying 'yes' when people offer kindness or support in large or small ways, whether someone is offering you their place in a queue or a family member is offering the chance for a baby-free nap. It's often much easier to give support than receive it, but you're equally deserving of any kindness that comes your way.

Feelings, like seasons, come and go. So as you ride those waves of loneliness, remember that it's not forever. Leaning on those around you and pushing into the things that make you feel connected with others will help soften the waves and welcome in smoother seas.

.... **TIP:** ....

Try to connect with others even
if you only have the energy to
engage in small ways each day.

....

See also:
Bored
Loud Inner Critic
Social Anxiety

feelings,
like seasons,

come
and go

loud inner

How I speak to myself matters

critic

The way you speak to yourself in the silence of your mind is THE single most important conversation you will ever have in your life. It dictates your self-esteem, how deserving you feel of good things and how well you feel able to accept support and love from those around you.

How do you speak to yourself? If it's tricky to answer that question, how do you respond to yourself when you drop a bottle of baby milk, or when you are late for an appointment? Do you respond with a kind 'Oh dear, these things happen!' or a critical 'Can't you do anything right?'

For many years, my inner chatter sounded like that of a bully. I found it hard to accept support when I needed it, let alone ask for it! I felt undeserving of my own beautiful baby because

he had no idea how much of a failure his
mother was. It turns out I wasn't a failure,
I wasn't a disappointment or a mess; those
things were not me, they were the narrative
in my mind.

And the good and wonderful thing about
narratives is that we can change them!

What would it feel like to speak to someone
you love in the way you speak to yourself?
How might it impact your little one's self-
esteem as they grew to the tune of those
words? Because, quite frankly, if it's not
good enough for them, it's not good enough
for you either.

Begin to recognize how you talk to yourself, how
you respond internally to what's going
on around you and what you do. You cannot

control this first thought, but you can do something with it. Don't let it get the last say on the matter! Begin to follow it up with a kinder, more compassionate narrative. For example:

First thought: *I can't believe I forgot my friend's birthday. How stupid.*

Second thought: *These things happen! It's not surprising really. My mind is so tired and I'm juggling a lot. I'm sure she'll understand.*

Sure, it might feel a bit silly, and it might be particularly tricky when your mind is tired and your energy low, but I promise it's a worthwhile investment of your energy, and you'll slowly see how beneficial this change can be. I can wholeheartedly say that addressing my internal dialogue has been life-changing for me.

TIP:

Write down some of the critical or impatient things you have been saying to yourself recently and imagine what a friend might say in response. Grab this list as a prompt next time you recognize that your inner critic is trying to have the last say.

See also:

Don't Feel Good Enough
Judged
Who Am I?

missing my

It's okay to miss what was good!

old life

When the attempts to meet even your own basic needs are hampered consistently, it's not surprising your mind wanders back to a seemingly simpler time. A time when if you were tired you could climb into bed early, or if you were hungry, you could simply eat!

Missing what was good about life pre-kids isn't a statement about whether you wish you could turn back time. It's an emotional acknowledgement that so much has changed, much of it in wonderful ways, but some of it in incredibly challenging ways where your needs – sleep, privacy and independence – feel like distant memories.

When we got the keys to our first house, we were overjoyed. Yet as we signed the mortgage, we truly recognized the cost of such a big life choice. Looking at the statement was a sobering reminder that we were in it for the long haul. Might we have had moments where we wistfully looked back at a simpler time when the heating broke and we could simply call the landlord, or when we booked a holiday without considering the hefty repayments we needed to fulfil? Yes.

But recognizing the cost doesn't mean it wasn't worth it!

There will be moments when you feel startlingly aware of the cost of motherhood. You're not ungrateful, you're human, and your resources are limited.

Expressing those moments where we dream of simpler days seems so taboo, doesn't it? Because we fear judgement or we know that those valid feelings may be met with a 'Just be grateful!' But the fact of the matter is that you can feel grateful *and* miss the easier breezier days when you could roll over on a weekend morning and listen to your body's need for rest, or when leaving the house didn't feel like a military operation.

When I've opened up about this with friends, I've often been met with a resounding sigh of relief as people felt the permission to be more honest about the greys of motherhood, and not just the socially acceptable sunshine feelings. Sure, some may judge, but perhaps that's because they're struggling to validate their own variety of emotions, or to understand them.

It's not ingratitude to miss what was good, or to find yourself dreaming about something that would meet a need right now (uninterrupted sleep, anyone?). In fact, it's human.

TIP:

Next time you find yourself missing
pre-baby life, instead of following
it up with guilt or judgement, simply
say to yourself, 'I miss some of the
good things, and that's okay.'

_____

See also:
Guilty
Self-care
Who Am I?

how I
speak

to myself
matters

need

**Needing space
sometimes isn't
'me first', it's
'me too'**

space

So you feel you need some space? Firstly, let's address the guilt that can so commonly come with recognizing that what you need most of all right now is some breathing space, maybe alone, maybe out of the house, maybe to laugh with friends. Either way, you need to step away for more than the two minutes it takes to pee.

In every other relationship we have in life, we know we need space, time away from that person so that we can return with a renewed sense of energy and gratitude for them. Yet when we have a baby, we can shame ourselves for not wanting to spend every single second of every single day, month, year with our offspring!

Your need for space isn't a reflection on your love for your baby, it's a recognition of a very basic human need for a sense of autonomy and that sometimes you need to feel like . . . you. Like your every fibre isn't needed, but belongs to you also. Like your full reason for being isn't to meet the needs of another, but to tend to your own needs too.

Needing space isn't 'me first', it's 'me too'. You might feel touched out, overloaded, tired under the weight of the juggle, overstimulated, understimulated. There are many reasons why you may feel a need to grab a breather, and there is no need to analyse it because it's just a human need that we should respect, acknowledge and accommodate.

So, how can you make it happen? Can someone step in for a little bit so that you can do something that refuels you? Can you utilize a local crèche or accept a kind offer from a friend? Then plan something in, be it a walk, a talk with a friend, starfish on your bed with a book, a baby-free browse around your favourite shop or a postnatal workout. Do you need a change of context or company? For inspiration, think about what used to energize you pre-baby.

Sure, the guilt may rear its head, but feel the guilt and do it anyway. If you're anything like me, that guilt springs from a false narrative that taking your space is indulgent, selfish. That you're fearing judgement from others, or that they might think you don't enjoy your baby. That you fear being a burden on the person who steps in to make it happen. But, trust me, the more you meet your very valid needs, the more you realize how beneficial it is for your mental health, and thus your baby will benefit from a mother who takes time to meet her needs too.

TIP:

How can you pre-empt your need for
space by planning it in advance? Diarize
it, make it a regular thing that someone
steps in for an hour or two – or three – and
you know it's there in your diary.

See also:
Overwhelmed
Touched Out
Who Am I?

overwhelmed

**Overwhelm hits
when we consistently
push through our
own limits**

Take a deep breath, deep down into your
stomach, and exhale steadily through pursed
lips. Drop your shoulders, soften your gaze and
move your tongue from the roof of your mouth
to the bottom. Where is the stress and tension
sitting in your body right now? What does it feel
like? What colour would you identify it as?

OVERWHELMED

Try to become mindful of these things as you continue to read and breathe through my words.

I know things feel heavy, suffocating even. The ticker-tape list of all the things you need to do, the responsibilities, the things you're holding in awareness, seems to be endless. I want to help guide you through this feeling of overwhelm, to gift you with some fresh clarity, perspective.

For me, overwhelm comes slowly, creeping up on me, nudging out my energy, my zest, my sense of humour and my feeling of being in control. I grapple to find more time, to do more, to be more efficient in the hopes I'll get to the end of the to-do list and find the sense of rest and calm that feels to be out of reach. As overwhelm takes over, I can't see the wood for the trees, perspective and clarity get replaced by feelings of irritability, indecisiveness, self-questioning, tearfulness, rage and a sense of claustrophobia in my own life. I feel increasingly sensitive to noise and guilty that even the happy noises of my home find me craving space. I feel misunderstood and alone, as if nobody understands the weight upon my shoulders. My metaphorical skin feels paper thin and I have little resilience to face the curveballs of life, which knock me deftly off my feet.

As overwhelm creeps up, we can often find ourselves wondering where the ease of our laughter has escaped to, or why even simple things feel like mountainous tasks.

Stop. Breathe. Let's review this right now. Grab a piece of paper and write down everything that sits upon your shoulders or heavily on your heart and we are going to put them into one of two categories.

1 The things you cannot control or change These are life's circumstances you find yourself in, the things you cannot control. These are the tooth emerging painfully, the nap interrupted by the doorbell, the family member who said something hurtful, or the lingering feelings after birth. You cannot change these things, but you can seek some techniques to help, a listening ear, or some good habits to support you.

2 The things you can delay, delegate or address What on your list can simply be taken off or delegated to another person or another day when you have a little more energy to tackle it? If you're like me, a perfectionist in recovery who takes great delight in ticking things off a list, then this can feel challenging. Remember, this is for now, not forever. Perfectionism can work against us when we are carrying so much, and lowering the bar at which we aim is an act of self-compassion, not an act of failure or defeat. You need to preserve whatever you can of your energy at this time, and cutting corners is a way you can store up some valuable resources.

What boundaries might you enforce to protect your energy? Can you create some temporary rules around what goes in your diary, your day and on your to-do list? It's exhausting living life when you've got little left to give and it costs you a lot. It costs the sparkle in your eye, the ease in your smile, and the energy in your brain to make decisions, to rationalize anxious thoughts and to coach yourself through challenging moments.

If you feel that you lean towards people-pleasing behaviour, that is also worth challenging. This is a time for you to receive from others. Friendship and love is so much more than spending all your resources on other people. You deserve to have something left of yourself so that you can be pleased too!

Finally, the main antidote to overwhelm and burnout is rest, which I know can feel like an impossible feat. See the 'Exhausted' section on p. 61 for some ways to get rest when extra sleep isn't really an option. Overwhelm likely crept up slowly, and therefore it will retreat slowly as you challenge and change what is within your power in order to gradually rebuild your energy stores.

·········· **TIP:** ··········

What change can you make today
that will help you recoup some
of yourself?

··········

See also:
Exhausted
Need Space
Sensitive to Noise

panicking

This moment will pass

If you are feeling panicky at this moment, I want you to listen to me. Imagine I have my hands placed on your shoulders right now. We can do this together.

This is just your body's fight-or-flight response filling you with adrenaline. We are going to breathe so that your body knows it's safe.

I know your mind might feel like a scary
whirlwind, but we can calm it.

Breathe. With me, in for a count of four, steadily
through your nose, all the way down.

1

2

3

4

Now, breathe out for six, through your mouth,
all the way to the end of your breath.

1

2

3

4

5

6

I want you to keep breathing like this, to calm your body. We can continue to switch off that emergency response as you read my words.

Your thoughts can be scary and powerful, but they are simply thoughts. They may feel very real, but I encourage you to look around you right in this moment. What can you see? What colours and patterns can you see in the space you're in? Now, feel the fabric of your clothes under your fingertips. What does it feel like? Can you feel the fibres? Next, I'd like you to notice the air passing your lips. Is it warm or cold? Have a listen to the noises around you. Not just the loud ones, the distant ones too. Finally, put your feet on the floor and feel the firm ground. These things are real, this is your reality.

I know it's hard to calm your body. I know it can feel like a battle to slow your heart. But as your body calms and your heart slows, I want you to be gentle with yourself. It can be so easy to respond to ourselves with frustration when we are scared, but you deserve patience and gentleness.

Take your time if you can. Grab a glass of water and take these next moments and hours slowly if possible.

TIP:

Perhaps later on, observe what needs
or feelings might have been lingering
under the surface of the anxiety. How
might you take a step to meet a need or
have your feelings heard and valued?
If these moments feel overwhelming
and frequent, please do seek support
via your doctor or therapist.

See also:

Anxious
Exhausted
Hormonal

procrastinating

Some things are better 'done' than perfect

Procrastination: that feeling when you know there's something you need to do, but for some reason you're coming up with all the excuses not to. It's getting repeatedly nudged to the bottom of the priority list, and feels like a weight on your shoulders you can't shake.

Hold that thing in mind. Name it, describe it. Whether it's a boring admin or household chore, an appointment that needs to be booked, or a conversation you want to have. What is it?

Now, consider the feeling you have about it. What is stopping you from wanting to get it ticked off and out of your hair? Is it that you are worried about doing it wrong? Sometimes the pressure we put upon ourselves to get something right can make it hard to face doing it at all, because we want to avoid the potential feelings of failure, guilt or self-criticism that may follow.

Perhaps you simply don't have the energy, because you're exhausted and that one job feels like a towering mountain to climb. Or is it one of those jobs that just feels relentless, like the never-ending washing pile, and by procrastinating you're claiming some kind of break? Maybe it's something you, quite frankly, don't want to do. Because it's scary, difficult, unpleasant or boring as hell.

Yes, consider the feelings you have, acknowledge them and name them. Don't criticize them or invalidate them, just notice them.

Now, consider an alternative. Is it something you *have* to do, or is it on your list because you feel like you *should*? Is it something you can delegate to another person so that it can be taken off the table entirely? Or perhaps you can postpone it to another day when you potentially have more resources to carry it out?

If it's something that does have to be done but it feels too mountainous, consider how you might break it down. If it's a long application form to fill in, aim for a couple of pages a day. Or if it's a huge washing pile, aim for one load. If perfectionism is stifling you, consider how you might lower the bar to make it less fear-ridden and more approachable. Because something done 'well enough' is better than it not being done at all because you've placed the bar at perfection. There will be plenty of time in life to do things well, but for now it's a kind thing to take into account the resources and energy levels you have available. If it's boring, how might you incentivize yourself? Perhaps you can watch your favourite programme in the background or pledge to walk with a friend after it is done.

⌐— TIP: —⌐

There is always a reason we don't want
to do something, or feel unable to face it.
If you approach your procrastination
with a kind and enquiring mind, you're
more likely to find a way to successfully
tick it off. Then you can sooner enjoy
that healthy, glowing feeling
of accomplishment.

———

See also:
Don't Feel Good Enough
Overwhelmed
Social Media Overload

some things are

better

'done' than

perfect

resentful

Just because your needs aren't understood, it doesn't mean they aren't valid

I'm so glad you're here. Honestly, I'm pleased that you've opened this page to explore resentfulness. Not because it's a bad feeling but because it's one that can get tricky when it's ignored. I know that acknowledging resentful feelings can feel uncomfortable if, like me, you've lived most of your life under the narrative that to be a good person is to always respond to people kindly and patiently.

The fact of the matter is that relationships are challenging, needs get overlooked, things don't feel equal, dynamics can be destructive, unhelpful and unfair at times. The load at home isn't always equally spread, the cost may be unseen and feelings misunderstood.

Here is my four-step approach to dealing with resentfulness:

1 **Why?** Can you pinpoint why you feel resentful and who you feel resentful towards? This feeling might have arisen due to lots of different situations or actions, or a general attitude over time. Resentfulness tends to involve a sense of injustice or

wrongdoing, enmeshed with feelings of humiliation, envy, being misunderstood or overlooked.

Perhaps my 'why' is that I'm resentful that my husband doesn't understand how much my life has changed when his seems to continue as normal. Yet nothing for me is the same, neither physically, mentally or socially.

2 **Which?** Which needs and feelings do you think have gone overlooked or unheard? Which behaviours have triggered this feeling of resentment for you?

My 'which' might be that I feel I am alone in the bone-tiredness. It has depleted me of energy and I feel jealous that my husband is just heading out for social drinks after work as I can barely scrape my own dinner together. He will probably wake me up when he gets home, making me more tired. So it's jealousy, feeling alone and that my need for sleep isn't being considered.

3 **What?** Now ask yourself what it is that you need. What would be your best-case scenario? What would be fair in this situation?

My 'what' is that I need rest, I need to feel heard and understood, and I'd like it to be acknowledged that the cost of parenting is different for me than it is for him. However, it would be fair to ask that he sleeps downstairs so as not to disrupt my sleep when he gets home late. And to ask him if he can take the baby on the weekend mornings so that I can catch up or go for a walk with a friend between feeds to feel sociable.

4 How? Now, how can you verbalize this or ask for these things? How might you talk this through in a constructive way? Perhaps agree to talk at a time when these feelings don't feel particularly triggered, not at a moment when the feeling of resentment is high. This will enable you to discuss it more calmly, and you'll be more likely to find a resolution together.

It can feel risky to do this, because when you put your feelings and needs out there, they may not be understood or acknowledged in the way that you were hoping. Remember that just because your needs aren't understood, it doesn't mean they aren't valid. Just because the feeling can't be helped, it doesn't mean it's not worth verbalizing it.

TIP:

Prioritize investing in the relationships
in your life to build a small network of
people (3+) who you can turn to, who are
affirming, kind and supportive. They might
not always be able to 'help' or fix things,
but they can validate and support you.

See also:
Feel Like a Burden
Overwhelmed
Touched Out

routine

**For many of us,
routine is the punctured
lifeboat we cling to**

anxiety

Oh, how I wish I'd known that routine anxiety was a *thing* in early motherhood. I don't know if it's officially a *thing* in any diagnostic book, but in my vast experience of talking to mums about anxiety and motherhood, I can conclude that it surely is a very common manifestation of anxiety.

I'm here to tell you what I needed to hear in those early months: that you're not 'just a control freak' and that there are reasons why you find it anxiety-provoking when routine is off-kilter. There are things you can do to navigate the feelings that arise so that you don't miss out on something lovely just because it means naps will be late or the risk of a car sleep is high.

Why do I feel anxious about routine?

While we humans are an adventurous breed, routine and predictability make us feel grounded and secure. It's easy enough to maintain routine and order pre-baby, unless a work thing crops up, or a rare curveball thwarts your plans. And then you have a baby and overtiredness, undertiredness, teething, colic, etc. send any semblance of routine out of the window for a while. Anxiety loves a focus, and routine was the lifeboat I clung to. Yet it had a puncture.

There is hope, of course, that your little one will settle into a predictable routine in time, but what about until then? And what about when the routine is disrupted? I have spent hours documenting wake and sleep times, grasping for a sense of control, hungering to see a rhythm emerge. I've had a phoneful of baby-tracking apps, and my heart has raced at a social invitation that will throw a spanner in the works.

There is also hope that you can loosen your grip on the need for strict routine to feel safe and grounded. Here are my tips:

- Focus on a small element of your own routine that you can control in a beneficial way. Maybe it's your own bedtime routine, or that whenever the baby naps at home, you do a ten-minute stretch and enjoy a warm cup of tea.
- Recognize when your anxiety is being triggered, for example when a play date is edging dangerously close to naptime. Anxiety is fear in action, so with

compassion, ask yourself what your fear is, what the worst is that can happen?

- Take each situation on a case-by-case basis. Question whether you could relax the routine in this instance. Relaxing the routine slightly might give you more opportunity to connect with another mum, or to arrive home less rushed and harassed.

- Your comfort zone may feel small and rigid, and this can be frustrating, but you are simply seeking a sense of security (and let's face it, most babies thrive on routine in time too!). Note when you're making decisions based on fear when, actually, even though it might feel uncomfortable to nudge the routine slightly, doing so will meet a different need, e.g. not rushing out of a baby sensory class to make it home in time for naptime means you get to ask the leader that question about colic massage.

·········· **TIP:** ··········
Next time you feel routine anxiety, ask yourself whether your decisions are fear-based or need-based. Seek support in the times you might want to nudge that comfort zone a few minutes out for your own benefit.
··········

See also:
Anxious
Judged
Winging It!

self-care

**Having a shower isn't
ticking the 'self-care'
box. That is simply
an act of self-respect**

Have you ever applauded yourself for:

- Drinking a glass of water
- Having a shower
- Going to bed at night instead of
  completing a box set on Netflix

- Eating a proper lunch instead of snacking your way through the day
- Going to the loo before realizing you've hopped past the bathroom ten times in the last hour

I used to applaud myself for doing these simple acts of meeting my basic needs, because sometimes it's hard to prioritize them when other needs shout (or cry) louder for my attention.

Until, that is, I recently had a light-bulb moment that totally shifted my goalposts.

Those aren't acts of self-care. No, those are merely acts of self-respect. My husband doesn't think he's engaging in 'a little self-care' as he hops into the shower or grabs a drink. Yet here I am approaching these acts with the indulgence and logistics of a spa day.

Your basic needs are to be fed, watered, clothed appropriately and sheltered. Even prisoners on death row get these needs met. If you ignored those basic needs required by your baby, it would be neglect. It would be damaging to their sense of self and self-respect.

How many times have I gone out without a coat yet spent ages deliberating over which layers to put on my baby? How often have I whipped up a lovely meal for my weaning infant while shovelling crisps into my face?

I know this is pretty hard-hitting, but I needed this to hit me right in the heart in order to start treating myself better. Everything you do for yourself is a statement of worth. These little things are immensely powerful in building your self-esteem or in sending you on a downward spiral.

Self-respect is meeting your basic needs. These are the things that bring you back to your base level. But as a mum, the calls on your resources have stepped up. You deserve more than functioning from your base level (or below).

The over-and-above are the things that are more likely to relieve you from teetering on the edge of overwhelm. The extra. The things that bring you back to yourself.

- It's not the hasty shower but the long bath with the bubbles you've never opened.

- It's not the gulped-down cuppa but scheduled coffee and cake with a friend.
- It's not the 'can you watch the baby while I shower', it's the 'please help me work out how I can get an hour or two'.
- It's not the message reply 'yeah I'm having a hard time', it's the 'can we talk?'

I'd love you to think about how you can find ways to give yourself more than the very bare minimum. Let those acts of basic-needs-meeting-self-respect be your non-negotiables, the foundation upon which you can add the gestures of self-esteem and resource-replenishing self-care.

TIP:

Write down three of your needs that
you can identify. Then write beside
them the minimal acts of self-respect,
and then the acts of self-care you
can engage in to meet them.
For example, 'I need space.'
Self-respect = getting out for a
walk to change context.
Self-care = finding a way to get a
couple of hours out of the house
baby-free with a friend.

See also:

Guilty
Loud Inner Critic
Need Space

sensitive

I'm not alone in having moments when the noises of my home make me want to scream

to noise

There are times when the noises in my home, even the happy ones, feel amplified. A chair scraping feels like it is reverberating directly in the core of my mind, or someone eating nearby can have me scrabbling to move to another room or flee the house entirely!

It's easy to feel guilty when you find even happy squeals or wails deafening. And I don't want you to feel unnecessary guilt! So here's why it happens . . .

When we are overstimulated, overtired, overwhelmed or hormonal, it can become harder for our brains to code the sounds around us as 'safe' or 'unthreatening', and instead they trigger our fight-or-flight stress response.

SENSITIVE TO NOISE

It may well be that the things that will help increase your capacity to process the noises around you are the very things that are tricky to find in early motherhood – space, rest and quiet!

I know it's hard to prioritize rest and space when you are constantly in demand, but think about how you might make this happen for yourself, even if it's in a small way. Noise sensitivity over your usual tolerance level shows that your body is in a state of overwhelm and stress.

I know it may be logistically tricky, and you may need to push through any feelings of guilt, but it's so important to acknowledge this need. You deserve more than to be in a perpetual state of stress. Noise sensitivity isn't a reflection of how much you love your baby, it's a human response to feeling overwhelmed.

Here are some small ways to refuel:

- Close your eyes for ten minutes to gift yourself some sensory deprivation.
- Listen to a guided meditation or some calming music.
- Give yourself some tech-free time each day.
- Take a quick (or long) walk round the block, alone if possible.
- Ask yourself what you need and find a small way to meet that need.
- Verbalize your feelings to someone, even if they can't help.
- Go to bed early and read instead of scrolling.
- Wear noise-cancelling headphones or an eye mask.

— TIP: —

Over the next week, jot down some of your trigger points for noise sensitivity and see if there is a pattern with how overwhelmed and overstimulated you were on those days. Consider what your needs are and how you might be able to soften the sensitivity by meeting them in some small way.

———

See also:
Overwhelmed
Self-care
Touched Out

social

**It's normal to take
time to find my feet
in new environments**

anxiety

If everyone who was feeling socially anxious had a little arrow above their head as they stepped into a new environment, or even a group of friends they knew well, then you'd realize how you were not at all alone in that feeling. We all just hide it oh so well (as you may hide it well too!).

Your heart rate picks up, you look around you, wondering how everyone else seems so at ease, you feel hypersensitive to what's being said. You are worried about whether you're speaking too much or not enough, whether you've offended someone or whether the laughter at your joke was fake. You're not alone.

I'm one of those who nobody would believe I had felt so socially anxious. I have perfected a facade of confidence over the years, whereas inside I've felt a wild tug of war! One part of me would want to stay while the other side was eyeing up the door or seeking a familiar person to stand beside like a human comfort blanket. I'd become extra aware of what I was doing with my own limbs, my hands became awkward extras I didn't know what to do with, and I'd fear I was talking too much to cover up my anxiety. While I still get these waves, they are fewer and further between as I've found things to help. There is so much hope that you'll grow in confidence too!

- **Remember that change is a transition** Having a baby brings a shift in your social life as you enter new environments, meet different people and engage in different relationships. If you began a new job, you wouldn't expect to know everything straight away, nor feel entirely confident as you stepped into the busy employee kitchen to make yourself a coffee. Newness feels uncomfortable as we are having to orientate our brains and our bodies amongst unfamiliarity (trickier to do when you're exhausted and finding your feet as a mum). See this time as a transition, because expecting yourself to feel as you felt pre-baby when approaching these things is a tall order.

- **Name it** If we feel able to name our anxiety, we will often be surprised by how many of those around us open up about theirs too. I recently walked late into a gathering of girls who were all sitting down, and I said, 'Oh my gosh, I felt so anxious there for a moment, walking up towards you lot!' There was gentle laughter of acknowledgment and empathy, and a couple of comments about people having felt the same. This put me at ease as I didn't feel the need to put on a confident face straight away, having given myself (and essentially asked for) permission to warm up. Many of us need a bit of time to warm up and feel at ease as we find our feet in different social environments.

- **Don't take too much responsibility**
  If you find yourself being the one who fills the silences, or takes the responsibility for keeping the conversation flowing, this can fuel anxiety. Most of the time, we are one half – 50 per cent – of a conversation, yet can find ourselves taking 90 per cent of the responsibility to carry it. Should that conversation feel awkward, or not flow well, we can end up feeling rubbish and at fault. When you recognize that you are

taking more responsibility than you need to, it means that those silences or one-sided conversations aren't about fault, but are merely the nature of human conversation.

- **Build up** If you feel anxious about entering a social setting, build up the time you spend there slowly, over a few days or weeks. Tell yourself you only need to go for fifteen minutes, or let the host or organizer know that you've got to dash away early. This takes the pressure off to be 'all or nothing', where you may push through the anxiety, feel uncomfortable, and not want to go again. Or you may decide not to go at all when actually it might benefit you in the long run. Ask yourself what would help. Perhaps you could ask someone to meet you beforehand so that you can arrive together, or phone someone you know who puts you at ease before you walk in.

- **Step away and breathe** If you feel you need a breather, or are feeling a bit wobbly, step away for a moment to breathe and ground yourself. Speak gently to yourself in your mind as you do so. You are finding your feet in a new environment, so it is completely understandable that you may feel waves of anxiety as you navigate that. You are not failing, you are feeling, and confidence is much more likely to grow when we seek or offer ourselves the support and patience we need, rather than criticize ourselves for being human.

TIP:

Ask yourself what might make you
feel more comfortable in this new
social environment. Then see if
you can enable that somehow.

See also:
Judged
Lonely
Panicking

social media

When we need to
retreat, we often
dive into the busiest
space of social media

overload

Our phones have become our support network, our admin centre, our diaries, our photo albums, our connection with the wider world, our entertainment, our workplaces and more. They are a throbbing, never-sleeping, ever-growing heartbeat in our hands. And you've probably flicked to this page because it feels like something you need, yet also sometimes want to throw out of the window.

Social media is an easy go-to when we want to escape something, be it a situation or a feeling. I've noticed such stark moments in which things have become tense, challenging or emotional in my home and I've reached immediately for my phone to scroll through social media.

Social media is a double-edged sword. It's full of words and images that will offer comfort, insight and encouragement, but also provides rich fodder for comparison, anxiety and overload. It is blamed for distorting our realities. Those shiny, tiny squares offer a version of motherhood we can't quite replicate. Well, maybe in a single image, for a moment. Our brains are hardwired to believe what we see, and it takes energy to rationalize that most of it these days is smoke and mirrors and filters. Unfortunately, energy is something we don't often have in abundance in early motherhood.

So, unless you plan on deleting all social media from your devices, here is my guide to using it in a way that will protect your mind as you scroll:

- STOP. As you pick up your phone, pause and ask yourself what you feel and what you need. If it's respite you are seeking or overwhelm you're escaping, you are about to enter the busiest, noisiest place in the world! How else might you use your phone to give you that respite or escape? Perhaps a guided meditation or texting a friend?

- Move apps to a different location on your phone so that your brain and fingers have to work harder to find them, buying you some time to think about the need you're trying to meet.

- When you are feeling vulnerable to comparison, instead of heading to social media, try to connect with friends whom you can be yourself around instead.

- Note how you feel when you leave your social media pages. Do you leave feeling educated, happier, fed, nourished by what you've seen, or low, rubbish and not good enough? Becoming conscious of the impact that it has on you helps you have more of a reason to control your usage.

- Consider how you might use your phone's control settings to help you become more intentional about how you use social media.

- Schedule regular breaks. Build them into your routine. I like to take Sundays off social media, and leave my phone in a different room at the start and end of the day to avoid temptation when my kids need most of my focus.

- Follow a variety of accounts. Use the mute and unfollow buttons to keep it a healthier space for you. You might feel more resilient to comparison in a few months' time, but while you're tired and your ability to rationalize is hampered a bit, be kind to yourself.

·········· **TIP:** ··········

Social media takes you away from
yourself, and the only way you'll ever
feel enough is by attending to the
very things you are neglecting as
you head there. What might these
things be and how might you tend
to them in a more nourishing way?

··········

See also:
Comparing Myself
Lonely
Missing My Old Life

suicidal

**Where there is help,
there is hope**

Imagine I am sitting with you right now, in this moment. Maybe perched beside you on your bed or next to you on the sofa with an arm around your shoulder.

Is there someone you can speak to now? Someone you can reach out to who will offer a warm, loving and calming voice? Please, make that call, you deserve the support you so often offer others. If you can't think of who you'd like to call, please call the Samaritans on 116 123, to hear a compassionate voice who will guide you through this dark wave. It can feel incredibly lonely and suffocating, but it will pass, and having a voice to hold you through it will help. You might feel lonely, but you don't need to be alone.

Look at your little baby, gaze into their beautiful face. Think ahead to the milestones, the giggles, the memories to be made both in the near and distant future. You brought this precious life into the world, and you deserve to feel the joy and wonder that is to come. If you feel like life is closing in on you and you're struggling to find purpose, know this: feelings aren't facts, because you do have purpose, and mothering your little one is a significant part of your purpose. Place your hand on your beating heart: you are here, you are alive, you have journeyed this far, and even though this moment feels dark and hopeless, the fact is that there are things ahead that will be too good to miss.

Think of the things that have carried you through your lowest moments. Think of the reasons you've held on through the storms of life so far. This desperate feeling, like all other feelings, will pass. This is a moment in time, a hard, painful, lonely and scary one, but it's a moment and it will pass.

If you're looking for a sign, this is it. I promise you there is hope that the sun can shine in even the deepest, darkest of corners. The morning comes after the night, spring follows the winter. Hold on and reach out, please. For you, for your baby, for those who care about you. There are better times ahead and, one day, you will reflect back on this moment and be glad you stayed.

When the moment has passed . . .

I'd love for you to feel a wave of immense pride that you walked through that dark time. If you can't conjure that feeling, I want you to know I feel incredibly proud of you. The pull can be so strong, but you walked towards life, and that takes strength you didn't feel you had. Now, I want you to think about what took you into that place. What was going on for you? What felt overwhelming? What were the circumstances? How might you put things in place should that dark wave swell again in the future? Are there decisions that can be made, or support you can seek to help ease some of the things that triggered that moment?

TIP:

When you are next feeling hopeful
and positive, write a letter for yourself
to read should you feel suicidal in the
future. Write warm and generous words
of support and hope. Perhaps you
can invite a friend or family member
to write it with you or write one for
you to tuck away somewhere safe
should you need a reminder.

See also:
Anxious
Baby Blues
Depressed

look at your

little

baby,

gaze into their
beautiful
face

tearful

**Crying isn't
weakness, it's a productive
and healing release**

So you're feeling tearful. Lovely Mother, let
them out.

These are emotions, your body's way of
releasing a feeling, a pressure, something that
has been held in. You might be 'mother' but you
are also a daughter, a lover, a person with
needs and feelings that respond to the world
around you. You don't always have to be on top
of everything, every job, every thought, every

emotion, every item on your to-do list. You hold a lot together, but sometimes you need to let some things go. And for now, if it feels appropriate, your tears are those things.

I know you might feel tempted to ascribe a reason, to rationalize them when they've begun to flow over something seemingly insignificant, but just respect this feeling. This is how you feel right now, and you don't always need to know why. You won't feel like this forever.

Imagine your tears as rainwater in the bottom of a glass. Crying is the release, the outpouring, and then they pass! What follows is space and clarity. Tears are healing.

I know that often our reaction is to hold the tears back, to swallow them down, to apologize for them, to hide them under glasses and excuses.

To see them as weakness and vulnerability. The truth is that vulnerability is a good thing sometimes; in fact, if vulnerability was a weakness, it wouldn't be so hard to be emotionally open with people! It's a strength. By letting the tears go you welcome a release of the happy hormones of endorphins and oxytocin.

Imagine the tearfulness as a wave or a labour contraction. It swells, peaks and then subsides. Of course, we much prefer the happier emotions, the joy, the gratitude, the mountain-top feelings, but sadness, grief and tearfulness, while they don't feel equally desirable, sure are equally as valuable.

If you feel a need arise as you turn your awareness to your tears, such as a need for comfort, space, talking or clarity, what might you do to honour and meet this need in a small way right now?

TIP:

Be aware of how often you feel tearful. It's understandable that your postnatal phase might bring with it some extra tears due to exhaustion, hormones and the recognition that so much has changed. But if you feel that your tears are coming much more often than you'd expect and they're impacting daily life, then please do keep in touch with your healthcare provider.

See also:
Baby Blues
Irritable
Overwhelmed

touched

**Wanting to sit on
opposite ends of the
sofa doesn't spell the
end of your relationship**

out

Crawled over, mauled over, hit, dribbled on, puked on, grabbed, bum-in-faced, carrying, hurrying, restraining, cuddling, wiping . . . as mothers, we get touched all the time. Those of us who consider ourselves tactile (pre-kids, I was one who revelled in snuggles on the sofa as we watched TV and I'd hug anyone who'd willingly receive one) can feel confused when we have babies and our desire to have physical contact changes.

We can start to question the depths of our relationships; partners might wonder whether our feelings have changed towards them.

I have found it so helpful to imagine that my personal need for physical contact is like a cup. I am happy when that cup is nicely filled, I feel a bit low when it's running dry, and if it's too full, it spills everywhere.

Pre-kids, it took longer to fill that cup because I wasn't in physical contact with someone all the time. A hug from a friend, a few handshakes with colleagues and a laze on the sofa were enough to have me content. These days, my cup is filled pretty quickly! And come the evening, I'm all tactiled out. My personal space has been so non-existent that I lean towards separate sofas and prefer to feel like I'm entirely alone when I sleep.

My husband, meanwhile, tends not to get touched at work much. A professional handshake, an awkward leg graze with the besuited man on the train. He is more likely to crave that physical closeness when he gets home.

So different!

And when our needs change and we don't acknowledge, verbalize or understand them, it can feel so confusing. We may fill in the gap with self-judgement and assumptions.

How do we navigate these differences?

1 Notice and voice them.
2 Know that this will change again as your baby grows and needs less physical contact.
3 Recognize your differing needs and understand them.
4 Talk about the assumptions you have so that the other person can clarify their feelings.
5 Make effort where you can, and get space where you need it.

∽ **TIP:** ∾

Keep the lines of communication open with your partner. Where there is a lack of communication, there are more likely to be assumptions, confusion and hurt. Be kind to yourself and explain and voice your needs and feelings.

See also:
Exhausted
Irritable
Overwhelmed

traumatized

**What I feel is more
important than any
diagnostic checklist**

As you read through this section on trauma,
go gently on yourself. I am not going to go into
depth on trauma but I want to offer you some
words of support, encouragement and hope.

The trauma I am referring to in this section
of the book is birth or pregnancy related.

Trauma can be physical, emotional or psychological. It is not just about what happened to you, it's also about how you felt as it did.

I have worked with women whose experiences of pregnancy or labour, on paper, may have appeared textbook; however, they felt anything but safe and supported. This is why it is so incredibly important to value your experience and not to compare it with the stories of others as it may prevent you from seeking the support you so deserve in order to help you safely process your feelings.

I think often we hope that the love for our child will override any feelings of trauma, and we might hold out in the hope that the feelings and fears will just ebb away as we bond with our baby. Let me reassure you that your trauma isn't a reflection on how much you appreciate or love your baby. Love can be a balm for trauma but not a treatment (of which there are many wonderfully hopeful and effective ones).

I also want to let you know that your response to trauma isn't your fault. It's certainly not due to weakness, lack of resilience or lack of ability to cope. Instead, it is caused by the way your mind has processed the event, sensation or feeling. How your mind processes things is down to a large number of factors which were out of your control at that time, because your brain was rightly focused on survival.

Imagine dropping your glasses on to the floor, and they are stepped on. The breaking and cracking of the lens is the trauma. Then you are left with no choice but to put the glasses back on so that you can see. You're now viewing life through the cracked lenses; they enable you to see, but the cracks are distorting your vision. This is the post-traumatic stress element.

Trauma is the event (or series of events), and post-traumatic stress disorder (PTSD) is the emotional and physical impact you experience as a result of that time. The wonderful thing is that with the right support to help you process what you have been through, those glasses can be mended and the painful memories can become integrated into your mind in a more comfortable way so that they are no longer the cracks that you see the world through.

I'd also love to let you know that it's completely understandable to feel a grief and sadness that

things didn't happen in a way you'd hoped or
dreamt they would. You can grieve the birth
you dreamt of, or the smooth pregnancy you'd
imagined you would have. Grief at the loss of a
hope is not a statement of ingratitude at the
final result of being able to welcome your baby
into your life.

Here are some symptoms of post-traumatic stress
disorder (PTSD). Please note, this is absolutely
not a definitive list, and the most important
thing is about how you are feeling, not about
how many things you tick off on any checklist.

- Flashbacks
- Anxiety
- Distress at anything that is reminiscent of
  your experience
- Physical sensations of stress and anxiety
  like pain, nausea or shaking

- Intrusive thoughts
- Nightmares
- Feeling easily upset or startled
- Using busyness, drugs or alcohol to numb feelings and avoid memories
- Blaming yourself for what happened
- Feeling irritable and angry easily

As I say, where there is help, there is hope. There are many treatment options available for you. I have worked with a lot of people who have experienced life-changing relief from the symptoms of post-traumatic stress. So, if your experience of trauma is staying with you and impacting your life in any way, please do seek support. You will find some onward recommendations in the Helpful Contacts section at the end of the book.

·········· **TIP:** ··········

If this section resonates with you, who might you speak to in order to take the next step towards relief from PTSD?

··········

See also:
Crying Baby
Depressed
Intrusive Thoughts

unsolicited

Just because it works
for someone else doesn't
mean it's right for me

advice

When you have a baby, suddenly everyone comes forth with advice on every single aspect. I often find myself metaphorically sitting on my hands when a friend is talking about weaning, sleeping or feeding, and even if they aren't asking for advice, I somehow feel desperate to offer my tips or experiences.

It usually comes from a place of compassion and kindness, but when the advice you didn't even ask for is coming thick and fast, how do you deal with it? There have been moments when advice has felt critical and questioning or has even had me wondering whether what felt right for me was wrong all along. But also some bits of advice given have been absolute game-changing gold!

I have a little two-step technique I like to use when offered advice:

1 **Respond kindly** Unless the advice has been offered rudely, is openly critical, harmful or hurtful, I tend to respond kindly. I might say:

'Thank you! I'll explore that.'

'I appreciate your advice, but this works well for us.'

'That sounds interesting, I'll ask my health visitor.'

'Ooh, that sounds good. Where did you read about it?'

'It's great that you found something that works for you, but we've been doing things differently and, at the moment, I'm happy with how it's going, thank you!'

2. Keep it or chuck it Now this is the good
   bit. It's where you take that nugget of
   advice or info handed to you on the street
   by the kind granny, or the friend with five
   kids, and you decide what to do with it.
   Metaphorically place that information on
   your palm and look at it. Ask yourself:
   Does it resonate with me?
   Does it fit with my intuition?
   Is it helpful?
   Was the source trustworthy?
   Does it line up with professional advice?
   Might there be something in it to
explore?
   Shall I tuck it away in the back of my mind
for another time?

And then you simply imagine keeping that nugget of advice or chucking it. If you keep it, you might act on it, research it or integrate it into your life. And if you chuck it, you can imagine wishing that person well, putting down that bit of advice and walking away (or throwing it swiftly in the bin if that feels therapeutic!).

⌒ TIP: ⌒

Remind yourself that just because
something worked well for someone else,
doesn't mean it's for you. And if it's not for
you, it's not because you're doing
something wrong, it's because you've
found your own way that works for you
and your baby.

———

See also:

Comparing Myself
Don't Feel Good Enough
Resentful

just because it **works** mean it's **right** for me

for
someone
else doesn't

unwell

Cutting corners is a form of self-care

Oh, the green-eyed envy I have towards my husband on the rare day he has called in sick to work and taken to bed. I have continued mothering through appendicitis, flu, stomach bugs and more. There have been many days I've looked at my bed longingly, my body crying out for me to crawl back under the warm covers as my baby cries out for a feed.

So how can you mother yourself through illness when you are mothering? Here are some tips:

1 Accept all help If it's available, take it. If you can call for it, call. As someone who feels guilty when a friend makes me a cup of tea at a play date, I know it doesn't always feel easy to reach out for support when you might just about be able to scrape yourself together and dose yourself up enough to carry on. But please, put that guilt aside, it's not justified. You'd do it for someone you cared about. Letting people support you is letting people love you in the way you love them. Feel the guilt and do it anyway, knowing that you're giving your body some of the much-needed rest it is asking for, whether it's letting someone drop a prescription round, watching the baby while you slow down, or letting you emotionally download over the phone. Accepting support where available isn't weakness, it's self-respect and care.

2 **Reduce your expectations** Do what you can to get what you need even if it means putting the rule book aside temporarily. You do not need to be guilt-tripping yourself right now, so amend your expectations of what you expect to achieve. Even if it irks you that the house is a mess and you're contemplating ordering takeout again, remind yourself that it's only for a while. Cut corners where you can. The more you take any opportunity to rest or slow down, the quicker you'll recover and the sooner life can resume in the way you like it.

3 **Type up your routine** When you're feeling well, write a detailed routine as if you were going away for the weekend and needed to hand over to someone who doesn't know how much milk your baby needs, or where the nappy stock is. It's

always a good idea to have this somewhere, so that the next time your temperature is climbing and you have the chance to retreat to bed, you can hand over the details and know that it will be covered.

4 Keep your medical box stocked up
We have teething salts and sticky liquid galore in our house! However, I've lost count of the number of times I've had to empty drawers and cabinets in the hunt for adult paracetamol. When you restock for the baby, do a check of anything you might need too.

5 Show yourself some kindness I bet you don't find it hard to tend to your baby with compassion and gentleness when they are unwell. You have exactly the same worth and value as they do. You are deserving of compassion and gentleness too in the way you treat yourself during this time and in the way you let others support you as you navigate your way through it. You might not be able to get what you need (a quiet weekend in bed, yes please!), but try to give yourself what you can under the circumstances.

TIP:

Type out a cheat sheet so that someone can step into your shoes (even if just for an hour) if needs be.

See also:

Guilty
Overwhelmed
Tearful

who am I?

Now is not forever

Every moment that passes adds something to who you are, even when you are sitting still on the sofa pinned down by a sleeping baby. To expect yourself to always feel acquainted with this current version of you at a time in life when everything is changing more often than the British weather is a tall order!

This is an incredibly intense period in your life, demanding so much time and energy. It can be tricky to see the wood for the trees when you're using all of your available energy and resources to help you find your feet in this new, ever-changing 'normal'. I remember finding it hard to even imagine a time when I'd not be dreaming of bedtime at lunchtime, or leaving the house laden down with a suitcase-sized bag of 'essentials', delayed by a poo explosion or another feed. But that time did come.

The things that make me feel like 'me' require energy! For me, they are laughing with friends, writing creatively, walks in nature, thinking clearly, reading good books, enjoying being with family. When I go through times of change or overwhelm, I have less available energy and fewer resources to engage in or enjoy these things. Books gather dust, words don't come easily when writing emails, let alone books, and I'm too tired to fight the anxious thoughts that draw my attention from being more present with those I love.

That energy will return, I promise you, as life settles into more of a rhythm. And don't forget, grief can come with change, not because you don't appreciate the stage of life you're at now, but because you miss elements of how you felt when you had freedom and energy in more abundance.

As you find your feet, I encourage you to think about those things that make you feel like you. What are they? Who are the people you can most be yourself around? What did you do for fun? What were you doing when you'd lose track of time and the rest of the world would turn into a blur as you engaged in this activity? How can you do small versions of those things for now? Find little nods to who you are that fit with your current energy levels!

For me, those things were listening to a few minutes of audio book as I fell asleep rather than force my tired eyes to read. They were to get out for a walk each day, even if it was a speedy trip round the block, and to commit to messaging or speaking to a friend or family member daily even if it was a quick text message. I would type disjointed creative thoughts into my phone notes, rather than sit at a laptop.

It's okay to miss yourself, it's okay to dream of a stage when you'll have more time and energy to do the things that make you feel like you. It's more than okay, it's entirely normal. Go gently on yourself: you are not gathering dust, you have not gone, you are just loving and living in a different way, and that's hugely productive in itself.

For everything there is a time, and motherhood isn't a time to wave goodbye to who you are. No, it's a time to get what you can for yourself that strengthens you and brings you joy, even if it's just a little bitesize chunk. Now is not forever.

TIP:

Make a note (in your mind or written down) of the things that strengthen you and bring you joy. How can you implement small things throughout your day or week that nod to those things?

See also:
Grateful
Grieving
Missing My Old Life

it's okay to

dream

of a stage when

energy

and feel like you

you'll have more

time

and

winging it!

Grow as you go

Imagine you're working in a job you know so well, and then suddenly you find yourself CEO of a company in an utterly different industry! Would you try to carry on as if nothing had changed, criticizing yourself for not knowing the ropes in this entirely unfamiliar territory? Or would you throw your hands up, admit to everyone that you've no idea what you're doing, and ask for help and support for all things, from where the loos are to the meaning behind the complicated office jargon?

I remember leaving the hospital with my first baby, placing the car seat in the car and feeling utterly amazed that we didn't have to sit some kind of exam before they released us. Did they not know that we had no idea what we were doing? We walked through the door of our home, placed his car seat on the floor and looked at each other. *What do we do now?* The more everyone around me seemed to know what they were doing, the more I feared they'd judge me if I let on how out of my depth I could feel sometimes.

I have spoken to thousands of new mums over the last few years, and the more people I've spoken to, the more confident I feel in the truth that we're all just trying to do our best with the varied experience and information we have. We are all feeling our way through in different ways, and growing as we go.

Here are some thoughts to support you along your way:

- Develop trust in your instinct. When you're questioning whether you're doing things right, ask yourself what your inner voice is saying. So often we look around ourselves or study what others are doing in order to validate our decisions and feelings. It can be helpful to look to others for advice and support, but don't completely bypass and overlook your maternal instincts and sense in the process.
- Babies don't need perfect mothers. The world isn't a perfect place, so as we are finding our way, whether in the moment you are winging it, internet searching it, thriving or just surviving, we are teaching our children that it's not about being

perfect, it's about leaning on the support
and knowledge available to help you
along your way.

- You weren't created to do this alone, and
it can feel very lonely when you're the
only one who knows your behind-the-
scenes reality. I often find that the more
honest I am with friends, the more they
open up too. When we let others see
behind our masks, we find connection,
and the shame we can feel about not
getting it right all the time can ebb
away as we are reminded that we're all
winging it!

- Perfectionism is an illusion. Sometimes
looking like you have it together is a
coping mechanism. Sometimes people
look like they have it all sussed, because
in that moment they do. Perhaps they
have good support, or lots of experience,

but don't be fooled that they don't have their wobbles or insecurities.

- Be mindful of where you go for information. As you open up a new internet search window, or go to message a friend, consider whether the information you might be provided with is trustworthy and grounded in fact.

- Take a moment to be proud of yourself! It's not always something that comes easily, but I encourage you to take a minute to reflect on the fact that this motherhood journey sure is a wild ride, and you deserve to recognize yourself for navigating it.

- Have patience for yourself. If you're someone who is quick to jump to self-criticism when you don't meet your own bar of expectation, think about how you'd speak to a friend. We often find it easier to extend kindness and compassion to those we care about, but you're deserving of that too!

·········· **TIP:** ··········

Note down five reasons to be proud of yourself. What would the you of five years ago think if she saw you now?

··········

See also:

Who Am I?
Information Overload
Unsolicited Advice

Babies

don't need

perfect
mothers

Final Note from Anna

Whether you have read this book through page to page, or hopped around dependent on what you need at the time, I hope that my words sink into your heart, introducing compassion and hopefulness. One of my favourite things to be told as a therapist is 'I had your voice in my head guiding me'. My own inner chatter over the years has been slowly transformed by the compassionate and kind voices of friends and my own therapist along the way. They've merged together to help form a kind of inner coach, one far kinder and more patient than what was there before.

This process has changed my life, and now I am able to give myself these pep talks in the moments when I need them. Not all of the time, but more of the time. My hope is that these words will also help to transform the way you mother yourself through the roughs and the smooths of motherhood. For we all need mothering, and if we can learn to kindly mother ourselves in the moments we feel most at sea, we will emerge from our motherhood storms a little less weather-beaten.

Not all of the time, but more of the time.

Helpful Contacts

I personally believe that where there is help, there is hope. And while that help may not always come in the shape or form you might have expected, there will be a listening ear somewhere who can provide that valuable sense of being understood, and guide you towards what steps to take next.

You deserve support and you deserve hope. So if you're feeling stuck, lost or overwhelmed, please do reach out.

Please note:

- The following guide contains UK contacts. There is a list of international mental health charities provided by The Calm Zone: https://www.thecalmzone.net/2019/10/ international-mental-health-charities/
- I have provided the website details for you so that you can access up-to-date contact information.

General contacts

Help Guide
https://www.helpguide.org/
Helping people make changes to help their mental health.

The Hub of Hope
https://hubofhope.co.uk/
Enter your postcode to find local support networks and charities.

NCT
https://www.nct.org.uk/
Information, support and classes for parents.

Postnatal-specific support

APP – Action on Postpartum Psychosis
https://www.app-network.org/
A charity for women and families affected by postpartum psychosis.

Association for Post-Natal Illness
https://apni.org/

A listening ear and friendly advice for any mum struggling postnatally.

The Breastfeeding Network
https://www.breastfeedingnetwork.org.uk/
Information and support about breastfeeding and perinatal mental health.

Maternal OCD
https://maternalocd.org/
Raising awareness and providing support for those touched by OCD.

Pandas – PND Awareness and Support
https://pandasfoundation.org.uk/
Offering hope, empathy and support for anyone impacted by perinatal mental illness.

Support for those feeling low, depressed or hopeless

Calm – Campaign against living miserably
https://www.thecalmzone.net/
A helpline for those in the UK who are feeling down for any reason.

Depressionuk.org
http://depressionuk.org/
A national self-help organization helping people cope with depression.

Mind
https://www.mind.org.uk/
Providing advice and support to empower anyone experiencing a mental health challenge.

The Samaritans

https://www.samaritans.org/

Volunteers available to listen every moment of every day.

Support for anxiety

Anxiety UK

https://www.anxietyuk.org.uk/

Help for anxiety, phobia, stress and anxiety-based depression.

No Panic

https://nopanic.org.uk/

Supporting people and carers of those living with panic attacks, phobias, obsessive compulsive disorders and other related anxiety disorders.

OCD UK

https://www.ocduk.org/

Educating, offering hope and supporting people through OCD.

Support in finding a therapist

The Counselling Directory

https://www.counselling-directory.org.uk/

A database of therapists and counsellors searchable by postcode.

NHS

https://www.nhs.uk/mental-health/talking-therapies-medicine-treatments/talking-therapies-and-counselling/counselling/

Details about counselling on the NHS and how to access it.

Professional Standards Authority for Health and Social Care
https://www.professionalstandards.org.uk/check-practitioners
Look for an accredited practitioner using the database.

Support for relationships

One Plus One
https://www.oneplusone.org.uk/
Evidence-based training and resources to support couples in strengthening relationships.

Relate
https://www.relate.org.uk/
Relationship support for everyone.

Support for families

Family Action
https://www.family-action.org.uk/
Practical, emotional and financial support for families experiencing poverty, disadvantage and social isolation.

Family Lives
https://www.familylives.org.uk/
Targeted early intervention crisis support for families who are struggling with family breakdown, challenging relationships and behaviour, debt and emotional and mental well-being.

Home-Start
https://www.home-start.org.uk/
Support for families with young children.

Pink Parents
https://www.pinkparents.org.uk/
Support and information for gay and lesbian parents.

Support for addiction

Al-Anon
https://www.al-anonuk.org.uk/
Support for families and friends of dependent drinkers.

Alcoholics Anonymous
https://www.alcoholics-anonymous.org.uk/
Confidential helpline for those concerned about their drinking.

Turning Point
https://www.turning-point.co.uk/

Support for those with drug, alcohol or mental health concerns.

Support for trauma and abuse

Birth Trauma Association
https://www.birthtraumaassociation.org.uk/
Support for those affected by birth trauma.

The National Association for People Abused in Childhood
https://napac.org.uk/
Supporting adult survivors of any form of childhood abuse.

Rape Crisis England & Wales
https://rapecrisis.org.uk/
Confidential support for women and girls who have experienced sexual violence.

HELPFUL CONTACTS

Victim Support
https://www.victimsupport.org.uk/
Independent and confidential advice for
victims of crimes.

Support for loss and grief

Child Bereavement UK
https://www.childbereavementuk.org/
Support when a baby or child of any age dies,
or a child is facing loss.

Cruse Bereavement Care
https://www.cruse.org.uk/
Support for those grieving after a loss.

Lullaby Trust
https://www.lullabytrust.org.uk/

Passionate about safer sleep for babies, and bereavement support for families.

Miscarriage Association
https://www.miscarriageassociation.org.uk/
Support for those affected by miscarriage, molar pregnancy or ectopic pregnancy.

Sands
https://www.sands.org.uk/
Support for those impacted by the loss of an infant.

Tommy's
https://www.tommys.org/
Support for those affected by premature birth, stillbirth or miscarriage.

Support for fathers

Fatherhood Institute
http://www.fatherhoodinstitute.org/
Training and information to support fathers and their families.

Postpartummen
http://postpartummen.com/
Support for men with concerns about depression, anxiety or other mood issues after the birth of a child.

Acknowledgements

The idea for this book came as I stood at the kitchen hob cooking tea for the kids on a Friday afternoon. Low on energy, I found myself searching my phone for someone who might give me a pep talk of solidarity to get me through the chaos of the next few hours. Wouldn't it be great, I thought, to have a book full of warm and supportive words to flick to right in those moments you need them? Words that spoke to the core of those motherhood feelings, words that comforted, grounded and brought clarity?

ACKNOWLEDGEMENTS

There and then, I typed my idea into my phone and pressed 'send' to my wonderful team at Bev James Management. Thank you, Bev, Tom and Serena. You completely *get* me. You get my heart and are always there to welcome my ideas with interest and consideration regardless of how wild some of them are!

And to my incredibly talented literary agent, Morwenna, thank you for welcoming my proposal with excitement, helping me shape it and finding me the best home in Penguin Life. Emily and Anya, my editors, thank you for choosing me and for echoing my passion for mums. I can't wait to share more ideas with you!

A huge thank you to my friends: Sam Powick, Kathryn Hogg, Kate Groom, Ella Dibb, Hannah Worlock, Sasha Wigley, Sarah Wharf, Rachel Balls, Marianna Osbourne. You all received the

book at various stages, offering feedback
and encouragement as I poured words out
(yet again) during the pandemic. You also
happen to be the most generous pep-talk
givers. Thank you for being who you are to me.

And to my mum, my husband, Tarun, and my
three kids, Oscar, Charlie and Florence. Thank
you for cheerleading me and for being proud
of me. Your relentless love for me has been a
catalyst for learning to love and accept myself.
And it has been fuel for the fire of my passion
to stand alongside other mothers as they find
love and acceptance for themselves too.